PLAN D

HOW TO DREAM, DRIVE AND DELIVER.
LESSONS FROM THE WORLD'S MOST SUCCESSFUL DISRUPTORS.

MIKE MADDOCK

Advantage.

PLAN D

HOW TO DREAM, DRIVE AND DELIVER.
LESSONS FROM THE WORLD'S MOST SUCCESSFUL DISRUPTORS.

Published by Advantage, Charleston, South Carolina.
Member of Advantage Media Group.

ADVANTAGE is a registered trademark, and the Advantage colophon is a trademark of Advantage Media Group, Inc.

Printed in the United States of America.

10 9 8 7 6 5 4 3 2 1

ISBN: 978-1-64225-090-9
LCCN: 2018967184

CREDITS

Managing Editor:	Paul B. Brown
Cover Design:	Bob Sprecher
Illustrations:	Wesley E. Douglas G. Michael Maddock Chris Miller
Layout Design:	Deanne Tyrcha

This publication is designed to provide accurate and authoritative information in regard to the subject matter covered. It is sold with the understanding that the publisher is not engaged in rendering legal, accounting, or other professional services. If legal advice or other expert assistance is required, the services of a competent professional person should be sought.

Advantage Media Group is proud to be a part of the Tree Neutral® program. Tree Neutral offsets the number of trees consumed in the production and printing of this book by taking proactive steps such as planting trees in direct proportion to the number of trees used to print books. To learn more about Tree Neutral, please visit **www.treeneutral.com**.

Advantage Media Group is a publisher of business, self-improvement, and professional development books and online learning. We help entrepreneurs, business leaders, and professionals share their Stories, Passion, and Knowledge to help others Learn & Grow. Do you have a manuscript or book idea that you would like us to consider for publishing? Please visit **advantagefamily.com** or call **1.866.775.1696**.

For my parents:
Nancy and George Maddock.
Thank you for your incredible examples
of unconditional love and faith.
Because of you, I am wonder-full.

Acknowledgments

I believe my purpose is to inspire and empower curiosity. I could not do it without the optimistic, caring, courageous, fun, authentic and wonderful people in the Maddock Douglas community—a community that includes hundreds of people who have helped us change the world over the last three decades. It is from this community that most of the thinking in this book was generated. Thank you all.

Special thanks to Ruthie Maddock (my wife), Stephanie Savage (my work wife), Wes Douglas (my work husband), Luisa Flaim, Cindy Malone and Maria Ferrante-Schepis (my work sisters), Gino Chirio, Charles Andrew and Randy Simms (my work brothers) and Paul B. Brown (my brother from another mother who just happens to be a fabulous writer and editor).

Finally, I want to thank my forum mates who have provided an unending stream of love, support and wisdom: Luis Balaguer, Pamela Blackwell, Rob Bond, David T. Brown, Greg Cohen, Jonathan Domsky, Thomas Elden, Tim Flood, Todd Gabel, Jake Geleerd, Brad Handelman, Jeff Hart, Todd Hatoff, Dr. Ari Levy, Edwin Lewis, Rob Lindemann, Larry Lineker, Mark Matuscak, David Mitidiero (RIP), Tony Perry, Frank Riordan, Tom Rivkin, Judd Rosenberg, Russ Rosenzweig, Marc Roth, Brad Serlin, Brian Weed and Bob Wolfberg. I am so grateful and so lucky to know you all.

With love and gratitude,

Mike

Table of Contents

Chapter 1
Here's To The "Crazy Ones"

Dr. Ari Levy stared calmly into my eyes and delivered the bad news. "The robots tell me you are fat." So despite years of hearing my mother say, "You look great, honey," it turns out I didn't. The robots don't lie.

That's right, the robots are coming (if they are not already here), and according to experts, by 2030, they will be smarter and more efficient[1] than us lowly humans.

This is the basic conclusion of the theory known as "technological singularity"—a state in which computers begin to teach themselves to be smarter and smarter, outpacing our measly brains in about a dozen years.

Today, it means that machines objectively report your muscle density and fat percentage. Tomorrow, it will likely mean that Dr. Levy—a doctor bent on disrupting health care—will be working alongside more robots than people.

The late Stephen Hawking and the very much alive Elon Musk both expressed concern about the unfettered rise of artificial intelligence, wondering whether the consequences will benefit or harm

---
[1] Probably skinnier too.

humans—a question that is hotly debated by the smartest humans I know.

Much of this hubbub is based on Moore's law, named after the founder of Intel, Gordon Moore.

In 1965, Moore made a prediction about what was clear to him would be the coming digital revolution. He had noticed that the number of transistors per square inch had doubled every year since their invention. From there, he extrapolated that computing would dramatically increase in power and decrease in cost at an exponential pace.

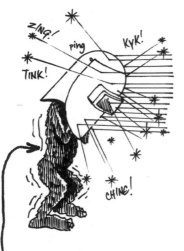

The extension of Moore's law is that computers, machines that run on computers and computing power all will become smaller and faster with time.

His observation has led a number of other thought leaders to believe in mind-boggling shifts that will be coming at us faster and faster; and if you look at the rate of change today, you have to conclude that they are correct. (Remember when you thought that sending a package overnight or receiving a fax was proof you were living in the "space age"?)[2]

Regardless of your opinion about artificial intelligence, robots or the pace of change, one thing is for certain: We are all now living in what feels like a science fiction movie—particularly if you are trying to lead, grow or start a business.

So how does a business leader keep up with the rapid pace of change?

Enter the Disruptor—the hero of our story. *That's you!*

"To be great is to be misunderstood."
– Ralph Waldo Emerson

---

[2] Today, immediate gratification takes too long.

As a young man, I liked to have money in my pocket. That meant that I took a lot of jobs and eventually manufactured my own ways to make money through entrepreneurship. Looking back, every one of my jobs—from ice cream scooper to furniture mover to laborer to designer—had me working for an entrepreneur.

They all worked, played, laughed, cried and lived too hard. I guess I shouldn't be surprised that most of them died too early. Like pieces of loud, grinding machinery, they ran too hot for too long. But man, they sure knew how to live—loud and large—when they were around.

And, oh yes, every single one of my bosses was crazy. But maybe that is to be expected.

Consider this from someone who is the poster child for Disruptors everywhere: Steve Jobs. The following is from the interview he did as part of PBS' "One Last Think" documentary.

"When you grow up you tend to get told the world is the way it is and your job is just to live your life inside the world. Try not to bash into the walls too much. Try to have a nice family life...save a little money.

"That's a very limited life. Life can be much broader once you discover one simple fact...everything around you that you call life was made up by people that were no smarter than you. And you can change it, you can influence it, you can build your own things that other people can use.

"The minute that you understand that you can poke life and...if you push in, something will pop out the other side, that you can change it, you can mold it. That's maybe the most important thing. It's to shake off this erroneous notion that life is there and you're just gonna live in it, versus embrace it, change it, improve it, make your mark upon it.

"I think that's very important...once you learn it, you'll want to change life and make it better, cause it's kind of messed up in a lot of ways. Once you learn that, you'll never be the same again."

WHOM THIS BOOK IS FOR

Thinking about my many Disruptor friends, I brewed up a strong pot of coffee and began to write a manifesto to describe their magical mojo. But after several attempts, it became clear that it had already been written by some creative guys named Craig Tanimoto, Rob Siltanen, Ken Segall and Lee Clow. They all worked for the advertising agency TBWA when Steve Jobs was looking to remake his then-struggling computer company.

In the late 1990s, Apple rebranded itself with the famously grammatically questionable tagline "Think different." The capstone of the campaign, created by those four guys above, was a TV commercial known as "Here's to the crazy ones."

The following is what you heard as images of 17 iconic 20th century personalities—Albert Einstein, Bob Dylan, Martin Luther King, Jr., Richard Branson, John Lennon (with Yoko Ono), Buckminster Fuller, Thomas Edison, Muhammad Ali, Ted Turner, Maria Callas, Mohandas (Mahatma) Gandhi, Amelia Earhart, Alfred Hitchcock, Martha Graham, Jim Henson (with Kermit the Frog), Frank Lloyd Wright and Pablo Picasso—flashed on the screen:

> "Here's to the crazy ones. The misfits. The rebels. The troublemakers. The round pegs in square holes. The ones who see things differently. They're not fond of rules. And they have no respect for the status quo. You can quote them, disagree with them, glorify or vilify them. About the only thing you can't do is ignore them. Because they change things. They push the human race forward. And while some may see them as the crazy ones, we see genius. Because the people who are crazy enough to think they can change the world, are the ones who do."

I literally get chills every time I hear Richard Dreyfuss, who did the voice-over, say those words.

Perhaps, not surprisingly, the words were originally inspired by this passage from "Dead Poets Society" starring Robin Williams:

> "We must constantly look at things in a different way. Just when you think you know something, you must look at it in a different way. Even though it may seem silly or wrong, you must try. Dare to strike out and find new ground.
>
> "Despite what anyone might tell you, words and ideas can change the world.
>
> "We don't read and write poetry because it's cute. We read and write poetry because we are members of the human race. And the human race is filled with passion. Poetry, beauty, love, romance. These are what we stay alive for. The powerful play goes on and you may contribute a verse. What will your verse be?"

Ironically, "The Crazy Ones" script was originally designed to be read by Robin Williams—a Disruptor in his own right.

So how did Steve Jobs originally respond to the ad? According to one of the creators, Rob Siltanen, Jobs loathed it.

"We played the spot once, and when it finished, Steve said, 'It sucks! I hate it! It's advertising agency sh**! I thought you were going to write something like Dead Poets Society! This is crap!'"

You can always count on Disruptors to tell you what is on their minds. Thankfully, you can also count on them to change their minds.[3]

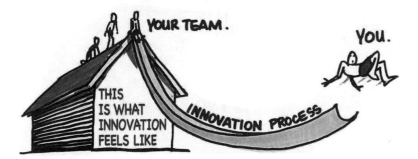

---

[3] Jobs ended up liking the spot so much that he was willing to read the voice-over himself. After they were unable to get Robin Williams to do it, and before they ultimately decided to go with Richard Dreyfus, Jobs recorded a version. You can listen to it at https://www.youtube.com/watch?v=cpzvwkR1RYU. See if you think it is as effective as I do.

For nearly three decades, I have had the incredible honor of working with the "crazy ones," the people who wake up every day with the intention of putting a dent in the universe—the ones who get things done. I've found them in the C-suites of *Fortune* 100 companies, in cash-starved startups and in third-generation family businesses.

Like many, I saw the dark shadows first. Working with and interviewing thousands of crazy people has revealed some traits that surprised me. At first blush, many of these habits and shadows may seem indulgent, crass or even frightening. But dig a little deeper and you will see that for every shadow, there is a brilliant light that helps illuminate change.

This book was written in honor of my Disruptor friends—the ones who are crazy enough to think they can change the world. My sincere hope is that this book inspires and empowers my friends as well as future generations of crazy ones. You are the Disruptors. And now, more than ever, the world needs you to do what you do best: Blow sh** up for the good of the whole.

Chapter 2

The Future. Disruptors. And You.

It is 3:30 in the morning and my heart is racing. I can literally feel, hear and taste blood as my heart beats through my chest. It is so loud that I wonder why my wife is still asleep. I am sweating. It feels like a freight train is tearing through the room.

But like every entrepreneur, I realize I am the only one who hears it. And I realize I am hearing it almost every night now. Every. Single. Night.

This is not good. This is bullsh**. This is embarrassing. Things were going so well a couple of years ago, and now I've once again been violently awakened by my lovely subconscious thoughts.

I know what it means. My reptile brain—the brain stem responsible for survival—has been convinced by my subconscious that a nice dose of adrenaline is just what my body needs at 3:30 in the freaking morning. It is telling me I must wake up and do something. Aaaaargh!

No wonder most heart attacks happen around 4 a.m.

As my heart rate subsides, I consider the dream I just had. As usual, the dream has a predictable central theme: Do I fight or do I run away from what's scaring me?

My subconscious sees something I don't want to see. I realize that my subconscious has now been asking me the same fight or flight questions for the past two years. But I have been ignoring the signals because when awake, my stress is manageable. I am in action. I am creating. I am selling. I am cheerleading my team. I am able to be blissfully naïve.

But when I am sleeping, there is nowhere to hide from what my subconscious already knows: We are in trouble. We are on the edge of survival. We need to do something different. It is time to disrupt our company or we will soon be disrupted.

I will tell you how this story ends at the end of the chapter, but let me give you some context first. And I'll tip my hand. EVERY SINGLE COMPANY—AND THAT INCLUDES YOURS AND MINE— IS IN DANGER OF BEING DISRUPTED.

Consider this:

- The world's largest taxi company does not own any cars.
- The world's largest media company does not create content.
- The world's most valuable retailer has no inventory.
- The world's largest "hotel chain" owns no real estate at all, not a single building.[1]
- Education has been reengineered by a hedge fund analyst.
- And a 16-year-old took down the record industry.

A few years ago, my company—Maddock Douglas, an innovation consultancy that has worked with more than 25 percent of the *Fortune* 500—coined the term "Napster Moment" to help describe something we were seeing happen to smart leaders more and more often.

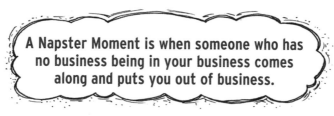

A Napster Moment is when someone who has no business being in your business comes along and puts you out of business.

---

[1] You know what else Uber, Facebook, Alibaba, Airbnb and Khan Academy have in common? Despite having a combined market cap of $675 billion—that's well over half a trillion dollars of value— if you are old enough to buy alcohol, none of these companies existed when you were born.

This is exactly what a 16-year-old named Sean Parker did to the record industry more than a decade ago, as you might recall, with his company that he called Napster.

YOUR YEARS OF EXPERIENCE

Napster was based on code the teenage Parker wrote to solve a problem the industry did not see—the growing desire people had to access music at any time, anywhere, digitally.

Because of the industry's blind spot, Napster became one of the fastest-growing companies of all time, amassing tens of millions of users within a year. And while it could not handle its rapid growth, its natural successor, iTunes, could—and the record industry as we used to know it no longer exists. By the way, iTunes doesn't produce any music.

The shift of power, customers and profit that Napster caused is almost impossible to quantify. This type of shift only happens when a Disruptor takes on a challenge and completely ignores the existing rules.

Is the Status Quo Your Blind Spot?

You may have noticed that Napster Moments are happening more and more often. You also may have noticed that many executives don't see them coming until it is too late. Just ask the CEOs of the hotel industry who laughed at Airbnb; or the taxi companies that are still trying to use legal action to stop Uber and Lyft; or the deans of colleges everywhere; or....

Is your company going to become a forgotten bit of history? Is your industry heading for a Napster Moment? Is your expert status at risk? Worse, will a Napster Moment put you out of a job?

The symptoms that your company—and you—are vulnerable are easy to spot: an inefficient delivery model; forcing customers to buy bundled services they don't want/need; the underserving of large parts of your potential market (e.g., millennials); or a cumbersome supply chain that is ripe for the picking. Do you see these symptoms? Or are you blind to them?

If you and your company have built the processes and culture to prepare you for uncertain futures, the symptoms above look like the start of an amazing race. Giddyup!

The vast majority of us have blinds spots that have been reinforced by years of knowing what worked and what didn't. We need to keep reading.

The reason the Napster Moment happened is easier to understand: 16-year-olds don't play by the rules.

Neither will the leaders of tomorrow's companies that upend other industries.

"GET OUT AND DON'T COME BACK UNTIL YOU HAVE MUCH LESS INDUSTRY EXPERIENCE!"

EXPLAINING TODAY'S BRAVE NEW WORLD

Long gone are the good old days where a potential sudden market shift was tempered by restrictive laws, huge capital requirements, industry secrets, detailed and complex distribution networks and expensive infrastructure. Today, "what's next" is conceived by firebrand leaders who barbecue the sacred cows of established industries. (See Chapter 5.)

It took Facebook **seven years to raise a billion dollars.**

It took Uber **five years.**

It took Telegraph—**a crypto play—just four months.**

Yes, the future is coming faster and faster. No wonder established companies are freaking out. (And no wonder they are increasingly turning to Disruptors to help save the day.)

HOW TO AVOID A PUNCH IN THE MOUTH

At this point, it seems appropriate to quote the surprisingly great—at least in this context—business mind of Mike Tyson who famously said, "Everyone has a plan, 'til they get punched in the mouth."

Right now, the future is punching businesses of every size and type in the mouth, unmercifully, and the blows are coming faster and faster. It took the pioneering Sears and Roebuck Company 59 years to reach a billion dollars in revenue. It took Amazon and Google a mere five years to accomplish the same thing. (Even adjusting for inflation, that's an impressive feat.)

Been to a record store lately? Dropped off any photos to be processed? Used a pay phone? Recorded an audio tape on a tape recorder? Used a video camera? Used a camera that wasn't a phone? Read an afternoon paper (or been able to find a local morning one if you live in a small or even midsize city like New Orleans)? Bought a printed map? Placed a call from your hotel room through the hotel's phone system? Ordered a set of encyclopedias? Rented a movie from a stand-alone video store like Blockbuster? Watched a TV commercial? Used a travel agent to book a simple trip?

Probably not.

The future already belongs to the Disruptors, and the rate of change is only going to increase. (For a list of industries—not companies—that are soon likely to be in trouble, see "Who's Next To Be Disrupted?" beginning on page 13.

Since 2000, 52 percent of the companies in the *Fortune* 500 have either gone bankrupt, been acquired or have ceased to exist. Yale professor Richard Foster, the man who founded the technology and innovation practice at McKinsey, projects that in four years, 75 percent of the companies on the *Fortune* 500 list will be companies we have not even heard of yet.

Today, the media is fond of talking about people like Sean Parker (who went on to become the first president of Facebook), Sara Blakely (the billionaire who founded Spanx), Richard Branson, Mark Cuban, Oprah Winfrey and Elon Musk. They often describe them as rule breakers or Disruptors. They don't need Ivy League credentials or your permission to take on any company—big or small.

And their minds work in ways that may surprise you. (Studying what they do to be successful could help you.)

In the past, when great leaders wanted to gain feedback, they looked to people who were delighted by their product or service. But when we deeply examine our most loyal customers and fans for insights into how well we are doing, we miss the opportunity to hear about the glaring gaps in our performance. While your No. 1 fan tells you what you want to hear, haters will tell you what you need to hear. Disruptors start with what people hate—something we will explore in detail in Chapter 7.

If you go to the people who absolutely loathe your product or service and ask them for feedback, you'll often find HUGE opportunities to improve your offering.

Disruptors start with hate (to innovate). That's the subject of Chapter 7. They also know that victims suck—the subject of Chapter 4—so they frequently turn your problems into their opportunities.

How? Well, they start by challenging convention (i.e., what everyone knows), such as: "Everyone knows you need a credit card or cash to make a purchase." There are a growing number of places that no longer accept cash. There is no federal law that mandates that you must.

Then they use frameworks to scale systems and memorialize wisdom, moving from "surreal" vision (self-driving cars...

are you completely nuts?) to sound strategy. Many Disruptors are more likely to build a platform than a product. (We will discuss this in Chapter 5.)

WHO'S NEXT TO BE DISRUPTED?
A GLIMPSE AT A DIFFERENT FUTURE

When it comes to disruption, let me give you three industries that I think are going to be in trouble very soon, to show you what I am talking about. I am only going to discuss three, but, honestly, I think it is harder to find industries that won't be in trouble than those that will. Most of us are going to see our industries and lives upended.

Insurance

Here you have a noble industry with an antiquated distribution model (agents, complicated paperwork) and outdated communication/jargon.[2]

Mavericks in this industry are working on making their communications more authentic, which means more understandable, down-to-earth, positive, credible, relevant and memorable. Equally important, they are working to find ways that consumers can interact with their products the way they want to. Think self-directed purchasing and/or customization of products and services.

One solution to winning in this vulnerable industry: If you can't build the change you need, buy it. The industry is currently investing billions in acquisitions and venture models.

---

[2] When you hear "protection," do you think condom or insurance policy? The defense rests.

Lending and Payments

If you have a great credit score and have had trouble getting a mortgage, you know how ripe this sector of the economy is for change. Add to that the growing number of "unbanked" people and the fact that there are too many hands in the consumers' pockets during just about every step of every financial transaction, and you understand the opportunity here.

True story: I recently gave up on refinancing our home because the amount of documentation required was a nonstarter. It was clear that it would literally take months to complete the process. My time is worth more than a half a point in interest. I suspect I am not alone.[3]

Enter crowdfunding companies and technology solutions that are able to fund things on smaller scales than banks and traditional lending institutions—or offer completely different ways to pay. Facebook is now in the payment business, following the lead of Square—another Disruptor that made it possible for anyone anywhere to take credit cards. (If you haven't experienced this firsthand, go to a crafts fair this weekend. You will see what I mean.)

One solution to winning in this vulnerable industry: Use data differently. There are plenty of ways to predict creditworthiness beyond credit scores, debt and income. In the future, these lagging indicators will be seen as marginally reliable at best.

---

[3] When they asked me for my sperm count, I decided I'd had enough.

MEDICAL, DENTAL AND VETERINARY CARE

These industries are ripe for change because of hassle factors, overly burdened providers, out-of-control costs, mistrust of insurance companies, and patients being at the mercy of inefficient models. Patients need to have more control over their care, costs and outcomes.

The changes here have been incremental: one-day surgery centers, emergency care facilities and the like. But the innovations are only marginally better than the ones that came before them. No one who has ever waited two hours in an emergency care center to be treated for an earache is going to say things are working as well as they could.

One solution to winning in this vulnerable industry: Stop asking the doctors and the vets[4] what the patients need. They will answer, "More comfortable waiting rooms" instead of asking, "Why do we make people wait?" Look for your solutions in companies and organizations that deliver unsurpassed customer service and empathy. Respectfully, too many industries try to solve problems by relying on the thinking of smart people WITHIN their industry. Not surprisingly, Albert Einstein got this one right when he said, "We can't solve problems by using the same kind of thinking we used when we created them."

---

[4] That's right. Dogs are people too—at least according to spending trends.

Your experts are too rooted in the past to conceive the solutions your customers will demand and get one way or another.

LEGAL SERVICES AND CONSULTING

You know how everyone has a joke about a lawyer or a consultant? If you own a law firm or are in the consulting industry, those jokes are nothing to giggle about. They are actually a sign of the growing frustrations related to process, costs, customer experience and complexity. These two industries are just entering their most disruptive periods in history.

As I said, this is just a partial list of the types of companies that may be in trouble soon. Accounting services are going to be upended; so, too, is car buying (even if you do your shopping online, actually "closing" the deal and being able to drive the car off the lot takes hours); college textbooks won't cost north of $100 in the near future. You get the idea. Yes, technologies like Blockchain and AI will drastically shift the fulcrum of power in all these industries— but they will be disrupted because people are not satisfied with the current experience.

AND NOW BACK TO MY STORY

The story at the beginning of this chapter is as real as it gets. Waking up afraid of imminent failure is a pattern that has happened to me like clockwork every seven years that I have been in business.

What I have learned from my dreams/nightmares is that the fear is being caused by subconscious realizing that there are some firms that have started nibbling around the edges of my business and others that have the ability to put me out of business with their new approach to what I do for a living.

I have also learned that I am not the only one having these (bad) dreams. Other entrepreneurs report the same thing is happening to them, and they tell me they long for the days when they could go seven years without them. They are occurring more frequently and accelerating as technology brings us the future faster and faster.

What they—and I—have realized is that each time we have these dreams, it is an opportunity to think differently, to reinvent and reinvigorate our businesses—to be the Disruptor.

This book is intended to be a road map of sorts. It will empower anyone who dreams of making a difference in their community, company or family. The chapters will serve as a checklist to follow as you try to create disruption of your own.

Why go through this exercise? That's simple: The best way to predict the future is to create it.

That's what Disruptors do.

Are you ready? Let's start creating the future.

DISRUPTOR TAKEAWAYS AND HACKS

1. **"Control your own destiny or someone else will."** Jack Welch–who turned General Electric into the world's most valuable company–said that decades ago during his tenure as CEO. It was true then. It is even truer today.

2. **You are either a Disruptor or you are going to be disrupted.** It is binary. There is no middle ground.

3. **We began the takeaways with a quote from a legendary CEO.** Let's end them the same way. Andy Grove–the man who in essence created Intel–was right when he said, "Only the paranoid survive."

Chapter 3

Disruptors Have Ghosts

To most people, Joseph (Joe) O'Brien seemed at the top of his game.

His company, RevivalX Capital, had reached No. 18 on the *Inc.* 500 list of the fastest-growing companies in the U.S. He had three healthy, rambunctious boys, and his beautiful bride, Mary, was always beaming by his side in the countless pictures that chronicled his success. Wealthy, healthy and smiling, they appeared to be living the American Dream.

But things were not as they seemed.

Joe lived a paradoxical, Jekyll-and-Hyde life. One moment he was a warm, genuine guy—someone gifted with movie star-like charisma who demanded attention from everyone around him. He could charm his way into the best seat in the house and make deals through persuasion and kindness. But beneath the smile, Joe was also ferociously rigid. And when someone violated a commitment, plan or principle, Joe would change into a manic street fighter. This moment of transformation was shocking and unexpected, even for those who thought they knew him.

Here's an example:

Once on a Colorado ski trip with Joe, back when he was just a casual acquaintance, I made the mistake of jokingly shoving snow in his face as we were waiting for others in our group. Joe snapped. He drove me into a deep snowdrift and began pounding snow in my face. He was sitting on my arms and I was absolutely helpless. My giggling quickly stopped as I heard Joe scream, "Say uncle! I want to hear you say you're done!" He meant it. Fearing he was going to hurt me, I quickly said, "Uncle."

Later that day, our group did an exercise, during which we each described the highs and lows of our lives. It was then that I learned Joe had an emotionally brutal childhood, which included his parents divorcing when he was young, schoolyard fights and ultimately being "sentenced" to an east coast boarding school hundreds of miles from his home because he was deemed unmanageable. His saving grace was his stepfather and eventual business partner, Jim. According to Joe, Jim stepped in and "saved me from myself," and then quickly talked about what a great life he had.[1]

At that moment, I came to understand Joe's Jekyll-and-Hyde behavior.

He was fighting his ghost.

MEET THE GHOST

I have never met a Disruptor who did not have a ghost.

Never.

We all have ghosts.

If you are a Disruptor, you'll recognize the pattern. The ghost appears in the middle of the night or in moments of uncertainty. The ghost is the voice in your head that tells you that you don't measure up to the rest of the class, even though it has been decades since you attended school. It is the whisper that informs you that your dad will never approve of you, even though you have outearned and outloved him by every measure. It is the secret teller that threatens to let the world know that you grapple with a mental disability like dyslexia or ADHD, which you've been trying to hide since you discovered it because you think people will perceive you as different and weak.

---

[1] As I've gotten older, I've noticed that people are really good at covering their pain with platitudes. #Guilty

It is the voice telling you that you are an imposter in your job, that you are completely outside your area of expertise, and someone—everyone—is going to find out. It is the righteous judge that tells you that you will never be rich enough, smart enough, skinny enough, funny enough, strong enough or clever enough to succeed—despite having the potential to be the most successful person your friends will ever know.

It happens to the most successful people everywhere. A good friend of mine organizes roundtable meetings for a top 10 global university so that the nation's brightest minds can share their ideas. In these private sessions, the professors are stunned to find that they share a common ghost: imposter syndrome. Most of them don't think they are smart enough to belong to such an elite group, which is precisely why they wound up in such an elite group.

When you control the ghost, your success is a dance between confidence and uncertainty. You may mock the ghost publicly and compete with it privately. Your ghost fuels your strategy to raise the bar and up your game. (More on this in a minute.) The ghost helps you be disruptive without hurting yourself, family or friends. You are going to show the ghost that everything he ever whispered was wrong (and, paradoxically, it is helping to drive your achievements and success).

But for disruptive leaders who are being controlled by their ghost, who believe what it whispers, things don't go so well because they fail to understand what is driving them. This lack of understanding has them desperately doubling down on their success formula: working more, loving more, fighting more, exercising more, buying more, launching more, partying more....

But those are not effective strategies because your ghost doesn't give a sh**. "You're still not good enough; you never will be," is the message it repeats again and again and again and....

For most disruptive leaders, ghosts appear early in life. Joe's childhood themes were rich in fear, betrayal and loneliness. They also certainly played a role in Joe's closely held secret: As an adult, he began to struggle with bipolar disorder—what was called being manic-depressive when he was growing up.

His childhood challenges manifested into a paradoxical blend of fear and possibility that drove Joe's business and personal life. His company bought the debt that collection agencies were unable to recover and then doggedly harassed debtors until they wore down and paid up.

While his company was collecting money, Joe was busy giving money away. He was known for his legendary generosity. He always had a stack of gift cards in his pocket so he could surprise anyone who exemplified good service. When a buddy asked him to make a small donation to a charity he had started on behalf of his daughter's illness, he said, "Sure," then quietly donated $6,000. Once Joe insisted on taking me to a Cubs game so he could introduce me to a friend who would become a cornerstone client—precisely when my company needed a new client the most. (Joe knew I needed help.) At about that same time, he introduced another good friend to a company that would eventually buy his firm, making him an instant multimillionaire.

Because of his childhood experiences, Joe never thought he would measure up. He saw himself as the "little guy" always fighting larger, more capable demons. As a result, he was always watch-ing out for the next business competitor, market force or villain. He made sure he found them everywhere—even when some of them were not real.

But there was a bright side. Joe's ghost empowered him to make a positive difference in people's lives, and he was happy to do it. Let me tell you a quick story about that.

When I heard about a collection agency coming after Geoff, a friend and workmate, I asked Joe for help. As Geoff tells it, he had gone to a mechanic to fix his car and the work had been botched. The mechanic was a bully and he billed Geoff anyway, eventually sending the unpaid bill to collection. Geoff was stuck with a car that would not run and the prospect of hiring an attorney he could not afford to fight what he saw as a clearly unfair bill.

Joe's reaction was simple and, not surprisingly, black and white. He said, "Mike, if Geoff has done nothing wrong, I'll help him. But if it turns out that he isn't being truthful, he's on his own." Three weeks later, Geoff received a very large check in the mail. Joe made it clear to the mechanic that he had violated the law and he was going to personally make him pay—pro bono on Joe's part—for messing with a friend of a friend. The mechanic was so scared of Joe's tone—and a lawsuit—that he sent Geoff a check well beyond the cost of the repair. I never heard a peep about this from Joe. Case closed.

For five years, I spent four hours a month with Joe in a business forum. Our group also traveled on retreat once a year—like the ski trip I mentioned earlier. In those meetings, we shared everything: our fears, our challenges and our dreams. Joe's central focus was always on his three boys. He was deeply committed to making sure they were protected and felt loved. He wanted them to have a better childhood than he did.

At 6:30 a.m. on a chilly September morning in 2006, I was driving on Highway A in Green Lake, Wisconsin, when I picked up a voice-mail from my buddy and forum mate Tim.

"Mike, I have some news. Please call me as soon as you get this."

My stomach sank. I pulled over and made the call. My worst fears confirmed: Joe was found dead in a hotel room. He had taken his own life.

The ghosts had caught up to Joe.[2]

---

[2] As you might imagine, I changed the names in this story out of respect for "Joe's" family. Sadly, the rest is as real as I can remember it.

LEADERS WHO HAVE THEIR GHOSTS

For many Disruptors, this is the most important chapter in the book. I included it and wanted to put it up front because I've seen what uncontrolled ghosts have done to friends like Joe. I've seen ghosts destroy families and companies, and I have wrestled with my own ghosts for a lifetime.

I'm not alone. And you are not alone if you are battling ghosts. As I said, I have never, ever met a highly successful person, someone who has changed the way business is traditionally done, who wasn't either chasing a ghost or being chased by one.

The central question for Disruptors is this: Are you chasing your ghost or is it chasing you?

The term "balanced leader" is often used to describe those of us who manage to inspire and empower our business associates, our family members and friends throughout their lives. After meeting with hundreds of "disruptive" executives, my take on this is that being "balanced" is only possible for those who manage to keep their ghosts in check.

In 2012, comedian and talk show host Jimmy Kimmel was asked to host the White House Correspondents' Dinner—a gathering on the Washington press corps and the people they cover. The highlight of the night for Disruptors was when Kimmel sarcastically addressed a former teacher.

"I also want to thank Mr. Mills, my 10th-grade high school history teacher who said that I'd never amount to anything if I kept screwing around in class. Mr. Mills, I am about to high-five the president of the United States." A delighted President Obama gladly obliged by high-fiving Kimmel, after which Jimmy finished by saying, "Eat it, Mills!"

Jimmy Kimmel wasn't talking to his history teacher. He was talking to his ghost. He wanted the world to know that he had his ghost in check. The ghost wasn't chasing him; he was chasing it!

When I started my first company, I pinned this quote from Theodore Roosevelt above my desk:

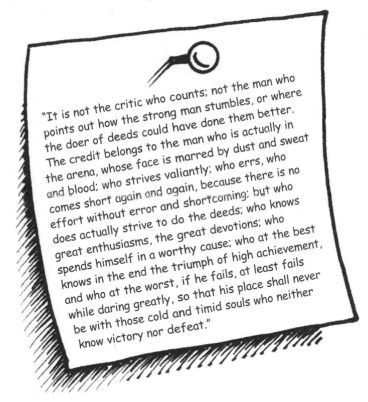

"It is not the critic who counts; not the man who points out how the strong man stumbles, or where the doer of deeds could have done them better. The credit belongs to the man who is actually in the arena, whose face is marred by dust and sweat and blood; who strives valiantly; who errs, who comes short again and again, because there is no effort without error and shortcoming; but who does actually strive to do the deeds; who knows great enthusiasms, the great devotions; who spends himself in a worthy cause; who at the best knows in the end the triumph of high achievement, and who at the worst, if he fails, at least fails while daring greatly, so that his place shall never be with those cold and timid souls who neither know victory nor defeat."

Today, I understand that what appealed to me about this quote is exactly what I wanted to say to the ghosts in my head. I would read it daily as a way to mock the voices telling me I would fail.

Eat it, Mills!

COMPETING WITH YOUR GHOST

Michael Jordan famously did not make the varsity basketball team his sophomore year in high school. He was beaten out for the last spot by Forest "Leroy" Smith. The event changed Michael forever.

Jordan developed a killer instinct as a result. Growing up in Chicago, I got to watch him in his prime and saw firsthand his reputation for being the most competitive person in the city. Whether it was basketball or golf, it wasn't enough just to win; he wanted to step on your throat and humiliate you.

Despite being the greatest basketball player of all time, Jordan never got over losing a spot on the team to Leroy Smith. Throughout his career, Jordan used the name "Leroy Smith" when he checked into a hotel, ensuring that if anyone called him, he was reminded of being cut from the team. When he was admitted to the Hall of Fame, he gave away 300 tickets. But he saved the last one, front and center, for Leroy Smith.

During his induction speech, he even mentioned Smith, telling his high school coach, "You made a mistake, dude." And then he said, "I beat you, Leroy. I got you."

Throughout his career, Jordan got better and better at basketball because Michael had the best scrimmage partner in the world: his ghost.

If you begin to journal about your nightmares, you will eventually see the pattern of fear being spun by your ghost.

Carl Jung, the founder of analytical psychology said, "Until the unconscious becomes conscious, we will be ruled by it and we will call it fate." So you need to understand your ghost to the extent you can use the fear as a constructive stimulus to create the outcomes you want in your life.

Put simply:

Be aware or beware.

Ironically, the "other" greatest basketball player of our generation, LeBron James, lists Michael Jordan as his ghost. Despite ending a 52-year title drought for his hometown, he continues to doggedly chase—or be chased—by Michael.

LeBron told *Sports Illustrated*, "My motivation is the ghost I am chasing. My career is totally different than Michael Jordan's. What I've gone through is totally different than what he went through. What he did was unbelievable, and I watched it unfold. I look up to him so much. I think it is cool to put myself in position to be one of those great players, but if I can ever put myself in position to be the greatest player, that would be something extraordinary."

Sleep tight, LeBron.

Identifying Your Ghost

A few years ago, I was on an executive retreat with 10 friends, all of whom run successful businesses. The idea was that we would learn from one another about how to grow our companies and deal with the challenges we faced.

John Drury, who became an executive coach after selling his advertising agency, served as our moderator. In an exercise that I will never forget, he asked us to list three adjectives to define the person we admire most.

"Generous, insightful and honest" is what I wrote. I was describing my dad.

Then John asked us to do the opposite: Think of the person we detest the most and describe him or her in three words as well. My negative adjectives were about a guy who had recently embezzled from our company. I wrote: "Greedy, oblivious, liar."

John then asked each of us to talk about the people we chose. It was at this point that the real lesson began.

Before the retreat, John asked each of us for the contact information for someone who knew us best. Unbeknownst to us, he privately contacted each person and asked: "What is his blind spot?" John figured correctly that the people closest to us would see something we may be missing.

After each of us presented, John pointed out that our positive adjectives were almost always the exact opposite of those we used to describe our villain. My case was the perfect example of opposite descriptions: generous versus greedy, insightful versus oblivious and honest versus liar.

But it got stranger. After pointing out the polarity of our examples, he opened a sealed envelope to read verbatim what those people closest to us had said about our blind spots. In every case, it was shocking how close each of us had described the people we hated.[3]

The lesson was simple: When we have a visceral, negative reaction to someone, we are usually fighting what we dislike most about ourselves. So when we are lashing out about things we "hate" in others, we might actually be fighting our own demons—our ghosts.

For example, at my absolute worst, as my wife (the person who knows me best and the one John contacted) points out, I tend to jump to conclusions. She said that at my best, I was insightful, but at my worst, I could be presumptuous (read: oblivious).

The best leaders have figured this out. They have learned to step back from moments of anger and be curious about what has them so upset. They notice that they are likely projecting that they are more upset about the worst in themselves than the person sitting in front of them.

---

[3] WTF? How did we NOT see that coming?

WHY DISRUPTORS ALWAYS HAVE GHOSTS

Dr. Jay Ferraro grew up in Brooklyn, New York, where he received his greatest education about dealing with ghosts and the resiliency of the human spirit. As an inner-city gang member, he learned early on to generate possibility in the face of violence, power and fear.

That led him to pursue a career as a psychologist, coach, writer, speaker and bodyguard to some very famous and powerful people. (Jay says he does this work to help feed his "inner warrior.")

So who better than Jay to talk about the ghosts of leaders?

Jay believes that it is often the dark side of the Disruptor that allows him or her to be disruptive; that genius always has a robust shadow; what some call a chip on your shoulder, and I call the ghost. His inherent bias as a clinical psychologist has him noticing this pattern everywhere anytime he is with a true Disruptor.

"It takes an inordinate amount of unusual ego strength to challenge the status quo, think out of the box, be a true entrepreneur,

speak the truth to power—and anyone else in your way," Jay says.

Ghosts are why Disruptors are able to differentiate and go solo against convention, logic and political correctness; truly innovate; engage in robust conflict; push back against the grain; and, in a word, be extraordinary.

Jay points out that the best-known "Disruptors"—people like Steve Jobs—are also the highest on the trait continuum of what his peers commonly call narcissistic personality disorder (NPD).

What is it? This is from Mayo Clinic:

Narcissistic personality disorder is a mental condition in which people have an inflated sense of their own importance, a deep need for excessive attention and admiration, troubled relationships, and a lack of empathy for others. But behind this mask of extreme confidence lies a fragile self-esteem that's vulnerable to the slightest criticism.

A narcissistic personality disorder causes problems in many areas of life, such as relationships, work, school or financial affairs. People with narcissistic personality disorder may be generally unhappy and disappointed when they're not given the special favors or admiration they believe they deserve. They may find their relationships unfulfilling, and others may not enjoy being around them.

Jay went on to list a constellation of traits that others may refer to as "narcissistic." These traits may well remind you of the darker side of a disruptive leader in your life. They certainly are reminiscent of some historical figures from the past and present:

1. Grandiosity with expectations of superior treatment from others. (They're perfectionistic, demanding and intolerant of the status quo.)
2. Fixated on fantasies of power, success, intelligence, attractiveness, etc. (They have a sense of destiny, self-importance, platform, uniquely qualified.)
3. Self-perception of being unique, superior and associated with high-status people and institutions. (They drive for significance, recognition, power.)
4. Needing constant admiration from others. (Self-worth = validation = "I will be loved, accepted and approved of.")
5. Sense of entitlement to special treatment and to obedience from others. ("I deserve it; and if you don't see that, we have a problem.")
6. Exploitative of others to achieve personal gain. (In other words, they operate via means-end thinking.)
7. Unwilling to empathize with others' feelings, wishes or needs. (They are self-absorbed to exclusion of context, thus miss others' experience.)
8. Intensely envious of others and believe that others are equally envious of them.
9. Pompous and arrogant demeanor.

Does any of that sound familiar?

We all have ghosts. The question is: Do you control them or do they control you?

DISRUPTOR TAKEAWAYS AND HACKS

1. **It is my strong belief and experience that to be disruptive and productive in all areas of your life**, you must constantly work on recognizing and managing your ghost. Start by naming it. Michael Jordan's ghost was named Leroy, his name for fear of failure. Jimmy Kimmel's ghost was named Mr. Mills, his name for insecurity. My ghost's name is "Boppa," after my grandfather who died with too many unfulfilled goals and dreams. Think about it. Who haunts you at 3 a.m.? What are they saying? What is behind their taunting? What is that outcome you fear the most?

2. **Compete with your ghost.** In the early days of my company, every time I felt an unfulfilled goal slipping away, I would read Teddy Roosevelt's quote on page 25. I would mock my ghost. It caused me to dig in and work harder.

   Michael Jordan found a playful way of competing with his ghost on every road trip. Imagine, he'd call room service and people would call his room to confirm the order using his ghost's name! He made sure he was messing with the ghost in every hotel.

DISRUPTOR TAKEAWAYS AND HACKS (cont.)

You may even consider creating quarterly themes or key performance indicators that tie directly to that chip on your shoulder. Feeling insecure? Great! Measure how often you get the right tasks done and give yourself a reward for it. Reward the exact opposite results that you fear the most.

3. **Be grateful.** Dr. Dan Baker, author of "What Happy People Know," taught me that it is physically impossible for your brain to be afraid and grateful at the same time. You simply can't do it. So when you feel like your ghost is getting the best of you—and you are afraid—make a list of things you are grateful for today. Read them aloud. Reflect on them. When you are being grateful, you always have the ghost, and it is impossible for it to have you.

DISRUPTOR TAKEAWAYS AND HACKS (cont.)

4. Make and keep a promise. Dr. David Fabry, a renowned hearing expert, lives under the shadow of imposter syndrome.

He was the first kid in his family to go to college. A gifted student, David began to receive letters of qualification early in high school, but when he looked into tuition, he knew his dad's salary at the paper mill in Green Bay, Wisconsin, would never be enough to pay his freight, so he was resigned to go to a community college or skip school altogether. Then the paper mill where his dad worked gave him three gifts:

- A scholarship to the University of Minnesota.

- A guaranteed union job during the summers.

- The chance to work with his dad and see firsthand how hard his father labored to provide for his family.

When David was 23, his dad died of cancer. At his bedside, David promised he would never stay in any job where he was no longer at his best, doing his best or becoming his best. His success in life, and with his ghost, is due to the fact that he has never broken his promise.

What promise could you make about your ghost?

DISRUPTOR TAKEAWAYS AND HACKS (cont.)

5. Helpful hardware plan. When I first started exploring the concept of a Disruptor's ghost, my wife, Ruthie, drew a biblical reference, commenting that it sounded like I was talking about someone being tempted by the devil.

John Venhuizen, CEO of Ace Hardware, saw a similar thread. John commented, "I'm a Christian, so faith is important to me. And, perhaps surprisingly to some, my faith guides me through this wrestling match. Intellectually, I am painfully aware of two things I detest about myself but know are true:

- I'm woefully flawed and the shadow sides of my biggest strengths are destructive.

- Left to my own inclinations, I naturally pursue my own control and comfort...often at the expense of a better path.

As a hedge against this, I use a simple framework that keeps me disciplined in this regard. The framework is I.R.A., and I learned it from a pastor about 20 years ago. It goes like this:

- **Input:** I need to regularly place myself at the feet of folks who have no vested interest in sucking up to me but feel entirely comfortable placing their foot in by backside when needed.

DISRUPTOR TAKEAWAYS AND HACKS (cont.)

- **Reflection:** I need to carve out time to be alone and reflect on my decisions, my behavior and my character.

- **Avoidance:** There are just things and sometimes people I need to distance myself from in order to avoid potential pitfalls.

John's I.R.A. framework is a wonderful way for leaders to remain aware and accountable. It also reminds me of John Wooden's quote: "Show me your friends and I'll show you your future."

6. **Look for angels.** JJ Carroll's mother was called Toni. It was no mistake that as a strong feminist she selected a gender-neutral name for her daughter. Toni would tell JJ that she'd have to work twice as hard as any man if she ever wanted to succeed in business or anywhere else.

JJ continued to seek her mom's approval years after Toni passed away.

Then she started to notice the smiles.

DISRUPTOR TAKEAWAYS AND HACKS (cont.)

It all started when JJ had to jump in to fill one of her mom's favorite roles at a family gathering—cooking. Since she had to feed a whole bunch of people quickly, JJ decided to make spaghetti. When she dumped the spaghetti noodles out of the pot, three remained, forming a smiling face. Startled, she immediately felt the warmth of her mother's approval.

From that moment on, smiley faces have miraculously appeared for JJ in moments when she felt particularly challenged and longed for her mom's loving coaching and encouragement. Smiles have come in the form of droplets of water on the counter, cloud formations, broken yolks of eggs, splotches on the road—even smudges on a computer screen.

By going out of her way to notice smiles, JJ now sees and feels her mother's approval all around her.

JJ is not alone. I've spoken to many leaders who use music, phrases and symbols to remind them of their better angels. And for leaders like JJ, it is working. Today she is the SVP of multibillion-dollar global company.

Chapter 4

Ouch, That Hurt.... Now What?

Imagine the worst possible thing. What would your life be like after that? Here's why I ask:

In the summer of 2017 at the Second City in Chicago, my wife and I went to see a one-woman show titled "She Came, She Wore, She Conquered...shoes, sex and other stories." It was written and beautifully performed by entrepreneur (that fact is going to be important here) Mikki Williams. The show was a bucket list item for Mikki and a gift for the audience. It also provided further evidence of something I'd noticed while doing research for this book: Disruptors simply refuse to play the victim card.

And Mikki Williams is a Disruptor—who could have easily been a victim.

Mikki was born and raised in New York City. Her mother, Bette, sold jewelry and kept the house in order. Her dad, Louis, was a furrier. Mikki's parents divorced when she was 4 years old, so Bette raised Mikki and, in the process, modeled what being a creator looked like.

She encouraged Mikki's individualism. She encouraged her to take risks and try new things. She exposed her to the arts, taking her to dance lessons, piano lessons and Broadway shows. When Mikki wanted a dollhouse, she took her to a hardware store to get sample wallpaper books and the materials so she could build the house herself. Bette never complained about being a single, unsupported mom. Instead, she worked hard, made her own money, and still managed to be waiting by the door every day when Mikki got home from school. When Mikki looked at her mom, she saw what she would eventually become: a strong, independent woman.

Mikki was a good student and attended Ithaca College where she met Gabe Durishin, who was attending neighboring Cornell University. Smitten, Gabe and Mikki were married just out of college.

For Mikki, this was the moment she had been waiting for... her childhood dream. As an only child, raised by a single parent, Mikki was lonely as a kid and wanted a "do-over." Her goal was to create the American Dream, raising a happy family in the suburbs. So although she started her career out of college as a professional dancer and a physical education teacher, she happily took on the role of a homemaker the moment she got pregnant with their first child.

By age 28, she was well on her way to her dream. She had a child and her husband was a rising star, first at helicopter manufacturer Sikorsky and then at IBM. Life was good.

Until it wasn't.

Mikki was pregnant with her second child when her father-in-law died suddenly in December. In January, she lost her second baby during pregnancy and almost died herself from peritonitis, an abdominal infection.

And then things got worse.

I think we all fear the knock on the door in the middle of the night. A month later, Mikki was awoken to that knock. When she opened the door, a police officer had come to tell her that her 29-year-old husband had died in a car crash while returning from a job-related event.

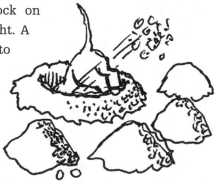

You could easily argue that Mikki Williams has been victimized by life. Her story is one that would leave most people cursing the heavens. I believe that what she experienced would send all but a few of us forgivably down a path of self-pity; a path that would ironically doom us to a self-fulfilling prophecy; a painful story fit for the Lifetime Network, Dr. Phil or a Jerry Springer segment.

But not Mikki.

THE CREATOR GENE

Just like every other entrepreneur I know, Mikki was born with the creator gene. And although she was punched in the face by the future early and often, she simply refused to play the victim. Her one-woman show was really about the inner dialogues she had with herself as she took on each of life's challenges. I suspect that it was these courageous conversations that had everyone on their feet at the end of her one-woman show and me crying like a baby during her performance.

Despite being a 29-year-old widow with a 2-year-old, no job and a mortgage, Mikki did what her mom had taught her to do. She created options.

She went from mourning one day to dancing the next. Mikki figured that teaching dance was the best way to make ends meet. She was so good at it that she quickly built one of the most successful dance studios in the country, one featured in *USA Today*. Her dance company performed on Broadway. She attracted famous clientele including Martha Stewart, Erica Jong and Joanne Woodward.

One of her students, Wayne Cilento, who was a member of the original cast of "A Chorus Line," went on to choreograph the show "Wicked."

But Mikki was just getting started. While her dance business was growing, she started The Happy Cooker, a catering business that Martha Stewart featured in her biography "Martha, Inc."

In all, Mikki created seven businesses, six of which were successful. She describes the seventh—a dancewear boutique called Kisses—this way: "That business failed me. It was profitable, but I wasn't passionate about it. I had better things to do!"

ALWAYS THE CREATOR

In 1987, Mikki decided to become a professional speaker. She wanted to travel, and it seemed like a good way to get paid to see the world. Today, she has spoken on every continent except one. "I refuse to go to Antarctica because I can't wear stilettos."

She was the first speaker to tour South Africa after apartheid, and she has spoken at the White House twice.

In 2009, Mikki fought and beat breast cancer. Always the creator, always the Disruptor, she threw an online tumor "coming out" party as a way to celebrate what to most people would be a private battle. Seriously, she threw a coming out party for a tumor.[1]

80% OF NEW ENTREPRENEURS ARE OPTIMISTIC — (Despite the fact that 66% of new businesses fail in the first 4 years.)

Today, Mikki is a business coach, chairing two executive peer advisory boards in Chicago for Vistage, where she was recently honored with their Lifetime Achievement Award.

Oh, and did I mention that she just started a speaker school and a speaker's bureau? In her seventh decade on the planet, it appears that Mikki Williams is just getting started.

We all have challenges in life. But I'll remind you here that this glorious story included the death of a husband, baby, business and having cancer, and Mikki still managed to make it a happy creator's journey.

---

[1] By this point, even cancer was an excuse to kick some butt. Bravo!

THE PRINCIPLE

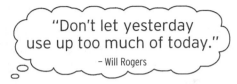

"Don't let yesterday
use up too much of today."
— Will Rogers

At one point, my friend Dr. David Zelman, founder of the Transitions Institute, was the psychologist to 3 percent of the world's billionaires. He rose to this level of popularity with the rich because of his unique ability to help people "transition" from one part of their life to the next. In the case of many of his highly successful clients, this meant from one successful achievement to the next.

David will tell you that you can't change the past. He will also tell you that you can't change the present because it is gone before you can do anything about it. The only thing you can change is the future.

Here is where it gets complicated and simple at the same time.

David argues that the ONLY thing that changes your future is the conversation you are having with yourself. He also says, profoundly, that he believes God's greatest gift to humanity is that we can literally change our world immediately—through the conversation we're having with ourselves about life's challenges and opportunities.

Like our Creator, we were born to be creators.

Disruptors like Mikki are aware and in control of the conversations they have with themselves.

Not surprisingly, Einstein had a clever take on this. He said, "The most important decision a man will ever make is whether he lives in a friendly universe."

This reminds me of one of my favorite stories.

Forty years ago, two shoe salesmen were sent to India to sell a new innovation: tennis shoes. After a couple of weeks, the sales manager called salesman No. 1 to see how things were going.

"This place is terrible. Nobody over here wears shoes!"

Concerned, the sales manager called the second salesman. His reply was completely different:

"This place is unbelievable! EVERYBODY needs shoes!"

Salesman No. 2 had decided that he lived in a friendly universe. He was controlling the conversation he was having about life's opportunities and challenges in a way that was generative and constructive.

So was Mikki Williams.

How about you? Do you choose to be a creator or a victim?

Who do you think made millions selling tennis shoes, the salesman who saw possibility or the one who was busy complaining?

VICTIMS SUCK

Here's the thing Mikki Williams and other Disruptors intuitively understand, something that many people miss: Victims suck. They suck energy, they suck possibility, they suck time…they rob themselves and the people around them of their ability to create a positive future because they are stuck complaining about the present or the past.

Put simply, if you don't want to suck, then don't allow yourself to be a victim.

As I said earlier, Disruptors like Mikki Williams refuse to play the victim. They opt instead to be the creator—completely in charge of bringing into being the outcomes they want to happen. They take full and unconditional responsibility for their reactions to life's challenges.

I often wonder if the challenge I am so distracted by today is going to make a bit of difference to me when I am old and gray. For the past decade, The Legacy Project has asked roughly 2,000 of the oldest Americans for their practical advice for living.

One question posed to them was: "What do you regret and how can young people reach the end of life without major regrets?" One popular answer: "I wish I hadn't spent so much of my life worrying."

Here's a great example: When Carnegie Mellon professor Randy Pausch learned that he had terminal cancer, he decided to make his final lecture about the most important lessons he'd learned in his life.

When things were at their worst, he found a way to create something beautiful; and his clear and thoughtful delivery left his family—and all of us—a timeless treasure.

As he eloquently put it, "We cannot change the cards we are dealt, just how we play the hand." So how do great leaders play the bad cards they are dealt?

When they hear themselves complaining about anything, they recognize they are taking on the role of the victim. And through this awareness, they quickly shift to a creator's mindset.

DISRUPTOR TAKEAWAYS AND HACKS

Here are three techniques I've seen my most resilient mentors use to successfully shift from victim to creator when faced with "a bad hand." These simple shifts allow the most resilient, impressive leaders I know to be courageous in the face of great adversity. Life's challenges lift them up instead of knock them down.

> *"Pain is mandatory. Suffering is optional."*
> —Haruki Murakami

1. **I wonder what this will teach me.**

    In 1648, poet Robert Herrick wrote in *Hesperides*, "If little labour, little our gains: Man's fate is according to his pains." In 1982, the exercise company Soloflex simplified this message with: "No pain, no gain."

    The people who have learned to look at challenges as valuable teaching moments are the wisest and strongest leaders I know.

    How do they convert pain into personal value?

    First, they understand that pain is always a temporary condition and an opportunity to learn. They ask questions like "How did I get here?" and "What caused this to happen?"

    They choose curiosity over self-pity or anger.

    Then they generously share their learning and experience with their friends. They commit to making the most of the opportunity for themselves and others.

    The next time you're faced with a particularly brutal challenge, ask yourself what you may learn from it.

DISRUPTOR TAKEAWAYS AND HACKS (cont.)

2. Reinvent your future—constantly.

"The key to success is to focus our conscious mind on things we desire, not things we fear."
—Brian Tracy

Choice is the enemy of fear. When you have choices, you don't feel trapped by your circumstances. We all have plenty of choices, but the most resilient leaders are masters at reminding themselves of this fact in the face of adversity.

When you are faced with a seemingly horrible situation, start by answering these questions:

- What is the outcome I most want?
- What other outcomes would be good as well?
- What stands In my way of making these outcomes happen?
- Who do I know that has overcome similar obstacles to those that stand in my way?

DISRUPTOR TAKEAWAYS AND HACKS (cont.)

3. Don't get furious; get (humorously) curious.

"Some people see the glass as half full. Others see it half empty. I see a glass that's twice as big as it needs to be."
–George Carlin

My friend Paul Landraitis loves to smile and exclaim, "Fascinating!" whenever a particularly troubling or unexpected situation arises. What's inspiring to me is that he does so with a laugh, choosing to look at every challenge through the lens of curiosity and humor.

I have two similar refrains when people ask me "How's it going?" (when it's not going very well). I laugh and say either "I've never felt more ALIVE!" or "I am living the dream!"

Both of these statements are delivered with a smile. Humor and context help me think more broadly and creatively. Both are absolutely essential for the best problem-solving, so I work not to take myself or my situation too seriously.

Both statements are also true. I AM living the dream (there are all kinds of dreams ;-). And when I am faced with a really tough challenge, I am the most focused...the most alive.

You may even ask your friends the question: "Can you tell me a few things that are funny about this particular problem I am facing?" or "What am I missing in my current situation?"

When they answer, listen for nuggets of truth and avenues for solutions and possibilities that you may not have ever considered.

Here's to wisdom.
Here's to the creator in you.

Chapter 5

The da Vinci Effect

As a student at Iowa State, Dan Heuertz was called "Hirize" by his friends. The nickname was born from his impossible-to-pronounce Luxemburg surname (roughly "High-Ritz"), but I think it stuck because Dan always had his head in the clouds.

Among other things, Dan dreamed about running world-class businesses. No surprise there. He was the manager of the Iowa State football team, he managed the Hilton Coliseum (the place where rock concerts and sporting events were held on campus), and he managed the bar off campus where I first met him.

I noticed that Dan was great at organizing his networks. Hirize was constantly connecting, and he seemed to know everyone. The people he ran into eventually worked together, played together and grew together. He ran a tight ship, always with a smile on his face and an organizational chart in his pocket.

Dan used his abilities of dreaming, managing and connecting to build a small business empire while still in college. He somehow acquired a defunct campus drug store and turned it into a live music bar, and then he used the proceeds to open a local keg shop.

His bar became one of the highest volume bars in the state and was named one of the best live music venues in Iowa. Meanwhile, the keg shop sold more kegs than any single location in the state. He was obviously paying attention to economics 101: beer and college kids = supply and demand.

Hirize's bar was called People's, and it became the place to be on campus for students and rock stars. The students were the easy part; Dan just let the ladies in for free and the guys naturally followed. In order to attract the rock stars, Dan leveraged his job as manager of the Hilton Coliseum. After each concert ended, he'd congratulate the performers, like Hootie and the Blowfish, and asked them what they were doing after the show.

"Dude, it's Ames Iowa," they would usually reply. "What do you do in the middle of nowhere?"

Dan was happy to inform them that he had a band kit and all the free beer they could drink waiting for them—along with their screaming coed fans—back at People's. They came, they drank, they entertained.

The after-parties quickly became legendary. Hirize was officially a Disruptor.

As you might imagine, his gift for organizing fun served Dan well after college. He started a bunch of restaurants, a credit card processing company, a consulting firm that worked to improve country clubs and their restaurants, a business coaching company...and today, he is busy building hotels in Iowa so that people can gather, bond and do business together.

It's funny how patterns repeat themselves.

From a distance, Dan's superhero power might appear to have something to do with bountiful booze, bonding and brotherhood.

But if you work with Dan once or twice, you will see the real key to his success: frameworks.

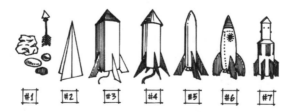

Ask Dan a question and he will pick up a marker, walk to a flip chart and begin to work you through the problem, using an organizational model—a framework—that he learned and tested while running a bar, a restaurant, a coaching practice or a hotel. Dan's ability to use frameworks helps him learn, optimize and repeat success. Coupled with the intelligence and the wisdom that comes from making mistakes, these frameworks literally make Dan a better businessperson every single day.

This is the perfect place to talk about why frameworks are so important.

SPEED OVER PERFECTION

> "Perfect is the enemy of good." – Voltaire

Leaders are made famous by their ability to make big decisions under pressure.

These "finest hour" decisions are often seen as make-or-break moments for sports teams, companies and even countries. Hollywood has immortalized these moments in movies like "Miracle," "The Wolf of Wall Street," "Saving Private Ryan" and, of course, "Darkest Hour."[1]

But here's a dirty little secret that most Disruptors grow to understand: More often than not, most organizations fail because they take too long to make *any* decision rather than making the right decisions. In other words, it is better to be wrong quickly than be right slowly.

Leaders who model quick decision-making empower teams that are able to learn, adapt, adjust and improve. And as the future comes faster and faster, the ability to make the best decisions possible—quickly—becomes more important every day.

---

[1] The movie deals with the first few months of Winston Churchill becoming Britain's Prime Minister.

In ending his speech to Parliament in 1940, where he pleads for them not to negotiate with Hitler but to fight him, the newly named Prime Minister says: "Let us therefore brace ourselves to our duties, and so bear ourselves that if the British Empire and its Commonwealth last for a thousand years, men will still say, 'This was their finest hour.'"

As the title hints, this (correct) decision plunges the country into a devastating war.

Disruptors make quick and courageous decisions, adjusting on the fly if the results are not what they hoped for.

Most people, especially most leaders, have problems with this approach.

The Genome project, conducted by leadership advisory firm ghSMART, tested 2,600 leaders and found that CEOs with the highest IQ often struggle with decisiveness. Their desire to get the answer correct often kept them from making any decisions at all. Not surprisingly, they also found that 94 percent of the tested executives who rated poorly on their decisiveness competency decided too slowly.

But for some, quick decision-making actually becomes a core value. Tony Lillios, the founder of Speck Design, described one of their core values as "stumbling forward." He taught his designers that teams learn best by being in constant action.

"By pushing our teams to constantly experiment, we naturally overcome fear and poor assumptions," he says. "Rapidly prototyping helps us create novel, unexpected solutions. It's the best way we've found to manufacture serendipity."

The U.S. Army also understands the importance of making quick, good decisions when operating in environments that possess volatility, uncertainty, complexity and ambiguity (VUCA). In fact, they use VUCA as a training framework to help leaders quickly make the best decisions under the most trying circumstances.

> **Instead of relying on gut or intuition, we need a reliable process to help us with our toughest challenges. The best Disruptors have one. They use frameworks.**

According to retired Brigadier General Bernie Banks, who now teaches leadership at Northwestern's Kellogg School of Management, "Under pressure, you want to be led by someone who is making the best decision possible, as fast as necessary. When you are being shot at, you need a mission-focused leader who can quickly move from mission to values to priorities to risk assessment to GO!"

So how do we learn to be like disruptive leaders and become people who make decisions quickly? We need to borrow the techniques used by Hirize, Tony and General Banks and rely on frameworks to help us navigate through our toughest challenges.

This chapter covers some of my favorites.

THE CHARACTER FRAMEWORK

Anyone who takes the time to write an essay titled "Fart Proudly" while he is busy inventing the stove, bifocals and odometer makes my list of favorite Disruptors.[2] But by far, my favorite Benjamin Franklin inventions were his decision-making frameworks.

When he was 20, he created a list of moral guidelines. He called them the 13 Virtues, which he believed were essential. Franklin would pick a different virtue to work on every week and make notes about the progress he was making.

Here's his list of virtues (the spelling is his):

Intelligence is learning from your mistakes.

Wisdom is learning from the mistakes of others. When it comes to innovation, wisdom is faster and less painful.

— GMM

1. **Temperance.** Eat not to dullness; drink not to elevation.

2. **Silence.** Speak not but what may benefit others or yourself; avoid trifling conversation.

3. **Order.** Let all your things have their places; let each part of your business have its time.

---

[2] Don't even try to cite Franklin's genius at home when you pass gas. Trust me; it doesn't work.

4. **Resolution.** Resolve to perform what you ought; perform without fail what you resolve.

5. **Frugality.** Make no expense but to do good to others or yourself; i.e., waste nothing.

6. **Industry.** Lose no time; be always employ'd in something useful; cut off all unnecessary actions.

7. **Sincerity.** Use no hurtful deceit; think innocently and justly, and, if you speak, speak accordingly.

8. **Justice.** Wrong none by doing injuries, or omitting the benefits that are your duty.

9. **Moderation.** Avoid extremes; forbear resenting injuries so much as you think they deserve.

10. **Cleanliness.** Tolerate no uncleanliness in body, cloaths, or habitation.

11. **Tranquillity.** Be not disturbed at trifles, or at accidents common or unavoidable.

12. **Chastity.** Rarely use venery but for health or offspring, never to dullness, weakness, or the injury of your own or another's peace or reputation.[3]

13. **Humility.** Imitate Jesus and Socrates.

When pressed about why and how they made a particularly tough decision, some of my favorite leaders will respond with a statement like: "It did not align with my values." Journaling and checking your actions against a set of values is a great way to make the right decisions for you.

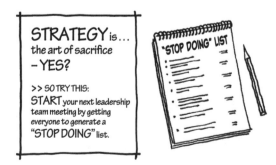

STRATEGY is...
the art of sacrifice
- YES?

>> SO TRY THIS:
START your next leadership team meeting by getting everyone to generate a "STOP DOING" list.

"STOP DOING" LIST

---

[3] Rarely? You gotta give him credit for word choice here.

THE DECISION-MAKING FRAMEWORK

Franklin had another framework that helped him land on the front of the $100 bill: his decision-making framework.

Here's how he explained it. It's not intuitively clear. Don't worry. We'll parse it in a second.

> "My way is to divide half a sheet of paper by a line into two columns; writing over the one Pro and over the other Con. Then during three or four days' consideration, I put down under the different heads short hints of the different motives, that at different times occur to me, for or against the measure. When I have thus got them altogether under one view, I endeavor to estimate their respective weights; and where I find two, one on each side, that seem equal, I strike them both out. If I judge some two reasons con equal to some three pro, I strike out five; and thus proceeding I find where the balance lies; and if after a day or two of further consideration, nothing new that is of importance occurs on either side, I come to a determination accordingly."

So in Midwest English, here is the process that Franklin used to make a tough decision:

1. Make your columns. The first should be titled "Consideration," the second "Importance" factor.
2. List everything you think important to making the decision.
3. Rate the importance of each consideration from 1–10.
4. Multiply the Consideration by the numerical grades for each.
5. Add up the totals and compare.
6. Make the decision.

Here's how this Franklin framework might look if we were trying to decide whether to acquire a company or build the capability organically:

	ACQUIRE			BUILD		
Consideration	Importance	Score	Total Score (IxS)	Importance	Score	Total Score (IxS)
Core values	9	6	54	9	9	81
Speed to market	5	10	50	5	3	15
Expertise	7	8	56	7	5	35
Cash required	3	7	21	3	5	15
Confidence of outcome	8	6	48	8	5	40
			229			186

Franklin's recommendation would be that we acquire the firm rather than build the capability.

Be Like Leonardo

Remember the game Mr. Potato Head? It turns out that Leonardo da Vinci enjoyed playing it. When doing a portrait, he would choose from various eyes, noses, ears ... that he had studied in the past. He used the same technique with gears, levers and wings. This simple use of a framework helped da Vinci quickly reapply knowledge and information across seemingly unrelated challenges. It was genius.

 The word genius has been debased over time. When we describe someone who can cook a great meal as a "genius" chef or a winning football coach as a "genius," the word doesn't mean much.

But Leonardo da Vinci really was a genius. He was a master painter, architect, engineer, sculptor, inventor and more. In every one of these disciplines, da Vinci approached his subjects with both novel and reliable frameworks. These frameworks helped him learn more quickly, invent more rapidly, and apply his thinking to a world of challenges.

The only way to excel in multiple fields—as we saw in discussing another genius, Benjamin Franklin—is to allow you to have frameworks that help you to constantly improve, see things others miss and move quickly.

Successful Disruptors use frameworks.

What I love about Franklin's decision-making framework is that it can accommodate both qualitative- and quantitative-minded leaders. It asks you to assign an importance factor about how you "feel" about a consideration and makes you apply a quantitative rank.

SMART GOALS

"What gets measured gets managed." –Peter Drucker

Although I am a fan of Franklin's decision-making framework, it does not ensure actionable results. (I can "know"—thanks to Franklin's model—that I should buy the resources I need, but it doesn't mean I will get around to it.)

To get into action, many Disruptors use SMART goals. SMART stands for:

Specific	A defined end point or target
Measurable	You track progress
Achievable	You begin with a goal that you can actually make happen
Relevant	You start with a goal that supports your broader strategy
Time Limited	It must be measurable over a specific period of time (i.e., it is not open-ended)

Using this framework is simple. When you establish a goal, test it against each SMART criteria, reframing the goal so you can measure progress.

Here's an example. This goal: "I want to finish writing this book quickly" might be modified to read: "My goal is to finish a 10-chapter, 45,000-word book about Disruptors by June 18."

The beauty of the SMART goal is that it helps answer the questions: "How much?" and "By when?" There is no wiggle room. As most of us know, just because we have chosen the right direction doesn't mean we've actually started the journey. SMART goals get you moving.

THE HAPPINESS FRAMEWORK

Want to live a long, fulfilled life? Perhaps Ikigai is the model for you. It has its origins on the island of Okinawa, home to the world's largest population of centenarians. Coincidence? I think not.

When I was asked to give a talk at a career day at the local middle school, I did a presentation on Ikigai, only I didn't call it "Ikigai" because I had no idea how to pronounce the word. Instead, I just called it the happiness framework. I figured that giving kids a framework for happiness first, career second was way more useful than talking about becoming an entrepreneur.

Here's how the happiness framework works. You draw four circles.

In circle one, you put what you love doing.

In circle two, you ask what you are great at doing.

In circle three, you place things people are willing to pay (big bucks) for.

And in the last circle, you put what you think are some things the world really needs.

Then you try to connect the dots. If you can get entries from each list to align, you will have just found a path that shows your purpose; your reason for being; something that will make you happy and provide you with a good income.

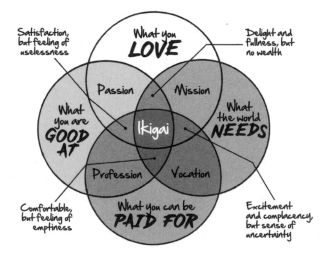

Here's an example:

- What you love doing: Working with animals and insects.
- What you are great at: Science and anything that requires a steady hand.
- Things people are willing to pay for: care for their pets.
- What the world really needs: More veterinary surgeons.

Veterinary surgeons are in more and more demand. They make an average of $185,000 a year.

I chose a simple example, but this same framework can lead you to unexpected jobs, like beekeeper, koi pond designer or zoo endocrinologist, simply by changing one of the criteria.

I think every high school should teach a course on the happiness framework. At the very least, it will produce a few people who actually know how to pronounce "Ikigai."

THE FIRING FRAMEWORK

"Do not tolerate brilliant jerks. The cost to teamwork is too high."
— Reed Hastings, CEO, Netflix

Intelligence is learning from your own mistakes. This means intelligence is painful, and it often leaves lumps and a bruised ego.

Wisdom, on the other hand, is learning from other people's mistakes. Wisdom is a gift offered by someone who has stepped in a pile of poop and is kind enough to tell you it is on the trail.

Since I've made so many damn mistakes, I often get to share wisdom.

I want to tell you about a time I stepped in something stinky and the resulting framework that I discovered—to help you avoid scraping a bad experience off your professional shoes.

The story starts in a surprising place— with me being forced to challenge something that I believe with all my heart.

That belief involves the very premise of this: Every company needs to be able to attract and manage disruptive team members.

These are folks who are brave enough to be truth-tellers. They question authority and convention. They offer unexpected ideas and challenge people to step up their game. They often see the world differently and have a lens that illuminates opportunities others might be blind to.

As I've said, Disruptors are absolutely necessary. The future is coming faster and faster, and a company must have disruptive thinkers in order to stay on its toes. No matter what you do for a living, someone—who may not be in your business today—is thinking of ways to put you out of business tomorrow.

You either prepare to disrupt or be disrupted. It is as simple as that.

So you need Disruptors on your team.

Even though there is no bigger believer in that idea than me, I now realize that hiring Disruptors *at the expense of everything else* is a huge mistake—and that's where I went wrong.[4]

In my quest for disruptive thinking and thinkers, I crossed a sacred line— the values that have helped make our company a success. And in the process of doing so, I did more damage to my firm than any competitor ever could because it crippled the company's mojo.

Now, I am not alone in crossing this line. But that doesn't make the lesson any less painful.

If you think about it, your employees fall into one of four quadrants. The performance matrix (used by leaders like Jack Welch, the long-term phenomenally successful leader of GE) helps explain what I did wrong. I've renamed it here as the firing framework to really drive home the point.

---

[4] Prepare yourself for wisdom. This retelling is going to hurt me way more than it hurts you.

The Firing Framework

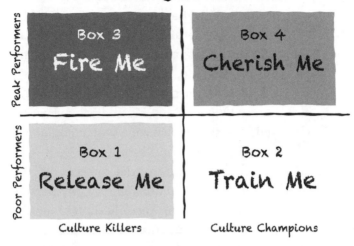

	Box 3 **Fire Me**	Box 4 **Cherish Me**
Peak Performers		
Poor Performers	Box 1 **Release Me**	Box 2 **Train Me**
	Culture Killers	Culture Champions

Let's deal with the two easiest quadrants first. There is no doubt about what to do about Bill, who is in Box 1. Release him. You made a mistake with this hire. He's not doing a good job, and he is violating all kinds of core values in the process. You must show Bill the door as quickly as possible.

Now meet Gary. He has been with the company for years. He is in Box 4, meaning he performs well and exemplifies what makes the company great. If you were to draw a person that best represents our core values, it would likely be Gary. We love and cherish Gary.

On to the harder decisions.

Meet Rebecca, who is in Box 2. True, she is underperforming; however, she is willing to work to get better, and you are willing to help her. If she does better, great. If not, it will be time to move on. But at the moment, she is a poor-performing work-in-progress. As someone who runs the company, I think the potential of training and coaching her outweighs the downside—today.

We now move to Box 3 and meet Ron. Ron is important to our company. Let's say he is a great salesperson. (He could be a brilliant marketer or strategist. Rons are found everywhere.) The performance of the Rons of this world may be driven by intelligence, showmanship, relationships, narcissism, unique market knowledge or simply a gift from the gods.

But the problem with our Ron—and maybe yours—is that he's a jerk. By this, I mean he consistently violates our core values—often  on a daily basis. (I am embarrassed to give you the details about what he did.) Here's the worst part: Everybody knew it, including Ron—and me, the CEO.

But, of course, I looked the other way. I called Ron (obviously not his real name) a Disruptor and stressed to everyone who complained about him that we needed Disruptors.

I told myself Ron was critical to the success of the company—and that he pushed us to think differently. My partners generally agreed. Besides, if he were gone, terrible things would happen to our pipeline…our profits…or our thinking…or our….

(This only empowered Ron to violate more company values.)

Most of us have made excuses for a Ron. Most of us have been afraid of losing him when we should have been afraid of keeping him around. Most of us have lost fed-up star players from Box 4 by not getting rid of him. At some point, they get so annoyed with Ron's antics that they leave. Many leaders count the hiring and the holding on to the Rons of this world as the biggest mistakes in their careers. I know I do.

The solution is pretty simple, although it took me a while to find it.

First, challenge yourself and your team to make hiring and firing decisions based on performance AND values. Each part is vital.

Second, recognize that although many Disruptors are jerks, it doesn't have to come with the territory.

And know this: If you don't eventually learn this lesson, you will, by definition, have put yourself into Box 3.

THE HIGHER YES

Diaphoranta is a Greek word that essentially means to focus on the essential, not the important. I learned it from my good friend Raphael (Raff) Vitón, a man who has thought deeply about how leaders prioritize. In my experience, great operators—the folks Raff and

I called Ringleaders in our book "Free the Idea Monkey…to focus on what matters most!"—are exceptionally gifted at prioritizing…at focusing on what matters most.

On the other hand, visionary dreamers—or the folks I call Idea Monkeys—are less gifted in this area, preferring to come up with multiple new ideas rather than focus on executing one or two. (We'll talk more about this delicate balance between Idea Monkeys and Ringleaders in Chapter 10.)

Now, some of the best Disruptors I've met are Ringleaders and some are Idea Monkeys. And in both cases, they have refined a skill that many people misinterpret.

Let's talk about Ringleaders. Here's some context first.

Unfortunately, we hear them saying "no" all the time. To many of us Idea Monkeys, we make the mistake of thinking the people who are saying "no" to us are just idea killers with no imagination; they were put on this earth to stomp on dreams, shrink budgets and dash the hopes of wide-eyed believers. We do the hard work of being ingenious, and they do the easy work of finding fault with our brilliant ideas.

(OK, I am obviously being dramatic to make the point.)

But great leaders aren't saying "no." They are saying "yes" to the things that must be prioritized, and they make that clear in turning down those of us who are disappointed.

"Part of our challenge is that we want to do it all," says leadership coach and former pastor Lance Witt. We can do almost anything we want, but we just can't do everything we want. So every "no" needs to be rooted in a higher "yes."

"The higher 'yes' is your purpose, your values, your calling and your talents. It's the 'must dos' of your life."

Witt continues so he can give an example: "Saying 'no' to staying up late to watch a movie could be rooted in the higher 'yes' of getting up to exercise the next morning."

Recently, a co-worker asked me if I could go to dinner with a client. She was on the verge of closing a really big deal. I told her that I'd love to, but I'd already said "yes" to going to my son's baseball game that night, so, unfortunately, that means I had to decline.

By pointing out to her—and myself—that I was making a value choice, I felt like I was supporting someone I loved rather than letting her down.

While we hear them saying "no," the best leaders are actually saying "yes"—yes to something more essential and less important. And if they are smart, they have learned how to make this clear to themselves first and us second.

This framework has particular value for service-minded leaders. We hate to say "no" to people who need our help. The solution is counterintuitive: Remind yourself and others that you have actually already said "yes" to something else.

THE PRIORITIZATION FRAMEWORK

So how do you prioritize your higher "yes"? How do you master diaphoranta?

It's an important question. As an Idea Monkey, I always have about two dozen more ideas than I can get to at any time. This drives me and my teammates nuts. When Raff Vitón was the president of one of our companies, he used to listen to me excitedly lay out yet another idea and then slowly and dramatically walk to a whiteboard in his office. He'd then write down the new idea...at the end of the long list of other ideas I'd put in front of him in the past. Putting the marker down, he'd calmly stare in my direction as he pointed at the board and ask, "Which one of these ideas is the most essential?"

To save my teams from the frustration that comes from creating long lists of important ideas, leadership guru Rand Stagen taught me how to use a useful framework that helps to separate the essential ideas from the important ones. I call it the prioritization framework.

Again, this framework is a simple 2 x 2 matrix. You simply place the ideas in a quadrant, based on answering the questions:

1. Does this idea produce high or low value?
2. Does this idea cost a lot or a little (time or money)?

PRIORITIZATION FRAMEWORK

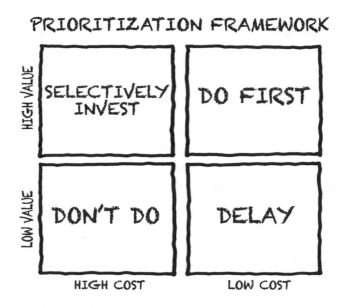

	HIGH COST	LOW COST
HIGH VALUE	SELECTIVELY INVEST	DO FIRST
LOW VALUE	DON'T DO	DELAY

As you can see, ideas that wind up in the lower left quadrant come at a high cost and produce little or no value. They are dogs. Admit that these ideas are among your least inspired and move on…to the lower right quadrant.

These ideas don't cost much, but they don't deliver much value either. This may be because of timing or some other factor that could change. So put off doing these ideas for now.

Now it gets interesting. The quadrant at the upper left contains ideas that produce high value, but they cost you a ton of time and money, so there are only so many of these you can take on at once. Pick one or two of these ideas (but as you will see in a moment, don't do that immediately). You must be very selective with this quadrant.

Finally, there is the quadrant at the upper right, the best quadrant of all. These ideas produce all kinds of value and cost you very little time or money. Jump on these ideas first!

Congratulations! You are now well on your way to mastering diaphoranta.

THE INNOVATION PORTFOLIO FRAMEWORK

As the financial markets crashed about a decade ago, CNBC's Erin Burnett and the late Mark Haines pressed me during "Squawk Box" to name a sector that would benefit immediately from focusing on innovation.

I responded without hesitation, "financial services."

Since the interview, the world has seen a plethora of new financial services and insurance businesses, models, products and services all fueled by the democratization of capital and data. Nationwide Insurance and Bank of America are now competing with Alphabet and Square for customers and relevancy. Blockchain is threatening to disintermediate everyone.[5]

What's perhaps most interesting about the reenergized sector is that it has used a staple of personal financial planning—asset allocation—to get dramatically better. Employed correctly, this approach will impact the future of your company with terrific results as well.

I'll explain.

When it comes to how you divvy up your personal investments, you have always been told that they should be spread among asset classes (stocks, bonds and cash) and then diversified further within the classes themselves. For example, you might hold stocks in both foreign companies and domestic ones, enterprises with large and small market capitalization, retailers and high-tech companies.

The idea is to capture all the potential gains out there. The more bets you place, the greater the chances you have of being right while minimizing risk.

You should use the same exact strategy when it comes to innovation.

---

[5] Disintermediation is a $20 word that describes what happens when consumers can draw a straight line between a product or service they want and the best supplier. This is awesome, except it cuts out all the middlemen. If you are one of the "middlemen," it kind of sucks.

THE FOUR CLASSES OF INNOVATION

So how would you divvy up your innovation portfolio? You have four choices.

I will list them and characterize what is good, bad and ugly about each.

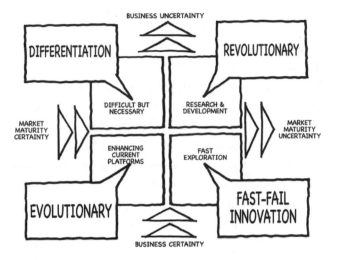

1. **Evolutionary Innovation.** It is technically easy for us to do, and we know our customer wants it.

   Included here are changes to pricing, simple line extensions and making small, incremental improvements to existing products and services.

   The Good: Your customers and partners expect you to be doing this all the time. It shows you are listening and you care.

   The Bad: This is like your money and market fund. There is very little margin in this quadrant, and your competitors are likely investing in the same types of ideas. You aren't going to make much money, and it does nothing to protect you from disruptive ideas or technologies.

   The Ugly: For highly conservative organizations—and leaders—this quadrant represents the entire innovation strategy, and it is eventually fatal: no margin, no imagination, no future.

2. **Differentiation.** It is technically difficult for us to do, but we know our customers really want it.

   This portion of your innovation budget is used for making a distinction between your products and those of your competitors'. Digital currency has been talked about and has existed for years, and now Apple integrates it into its phones. The trick here is to move from buzzwords (e.g., blockchain, AI, IOT) to finding real ways to solve today's customer challenges with the technology.

   The Good: Do this right and you create a culture that knows how to figure out challenges related directly to consumer need, resulting in higher margins and more engaged customers.

   The Bad: Often, conservative companies will over test and diminish new ideas to the point of being late to the market or, worse, launching something that is so safe that it lacks the sizzle to make the market take notice.

   The Ugly: In conservative companies, this is where your best Disruptors go to die. They get so tired of trudging through both fear and slow, overly conservative processes that they leave.

3. **Revolutionary Innovation.** It seems technically impossible to do; but even if we can do it, there's no way of knowing ahead of time if anyone will buy it.

   This is the place where you search to find groundbreaking ideas for products, services and business models. PayPal, Uber, Nest and Fitbit are examples of "crazy" ideas that started in this quadrant. Here, you are making a bet that the market will move toward your idea, and your company will have a first-mover advantage.

   The Good: This is the most inspiring quadrant for your team. Companies that get this quadrant right literally transform industries and gain enormous increases in margin and market share.

   The Bad: Investments in this quadrant rarely pay off and are extremely difficult and costly to forecast.

The Ugly: If you invest too heavily in this quadrant, you will lose the faith of the market and bankrupt your company. Also, if you are like most mature companies, your team is perfectly engineered to kill any idea that comes from this quadrant. More on this later.

4. **Fast-Fail Innovation.** It is technically easy for us to do, but we have no idea if anyone will buy it.

   This is the playground of the Idea Monkeys and entrepreneurial startups. Here you must go to market and quickly test and learn. It is the opportunistic segment of your development activity (i.e., it is well within your wheelhouse of capabilities and core competencies but far more experimental than usual).

   Here you expect to fail quickly before succeeding with an offering that may literally be refined by your customers' feedback in the market.

   The Fast-Fail Innovation quadrant is fairly low risk (you don't spend much before you send the product out into the marketplace), and it has an extremely high potential reward as customers express exactly how they want you to alter it.

   The direct response marketing industry has been using this strategy for decades, testing products like the Snuggie, OxiClean and Total Gym in small markets before rolling them out nationally once they incorporate market feedback and show traction.

   The Good: This quadrant is a great outlet for your imaginative, entrepreneurial thinkers—low risk and low cost with potential for high returns. I mean, who doesn't like a good hackathon or brainstorm in the morning?

   The Bad: This quadrant can be a distraction. Overinvestment here often signals a lack of discipline or an inability to gather insights. Fact: Large innovation returns depend on large market needs.

   The Ugly: Entrepreneurs, on average, are out of business in fewer than three years because they overinvest in this strategy. They run out of time and money because they are focused on too many ideas at once.

WHAT IS THE RIGHT PORTFOLIO FOR YOU?

So what might your portfolio look like?

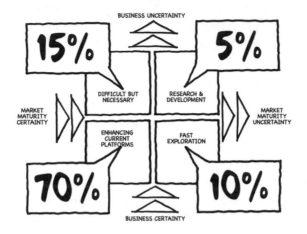

In more aggressive industries (i.e., industries such as consumer electronics that live and die on new products), your innovation portfolio development model might see more efforts in the upper right side of the diagram and less in the lower left. In more conservative industries, it's vice versa. Regardless of the industry, the right balance can yield billions in results.

A HIDDEN BENEFIT

The nice thing about approaching innovation this way is that it reduces the subjective approach companies have to funding innovation. You have your innovation asset allocation model and you divide your money and time up accordingly. It reduces the stress at budget time by getting everyone thinking the same way about how to set priorities.

It also gives Disruptors in your organization a place to play. And in doing so, it allows the other people to do the solid work your company needs today and tomorrow while the Disruptors are busy working on what you'll need three years from now.

And there is an even more important benefit: A balanced portfolio reflects a culture that knows how to create seeds of ideas and grow them. Show me a balanced portfolio and I'll show you a culture that can innovate again and again.

OUTSOURCE YOUR CRAZY

Some quick portfolio guidance, which I mentioned in passing in this chapter: After nearly three decades of working with solid, mature companies, I can tell you that they are perfectly engineered to kill any idea that threatens their legacy products and services.

Evolved leaders do not feel bad about this; they are proud of it. They have built companies that are designed to improve what they are doing today by just a little bit tomorrow.

This is a good thing. It is what your people were hired to do and what your ecosystem is designed to do.

For this reason, I strongly suggest that you "outsource" your most revolutionary ideas vis-à-vis a separate location, team or venture model. The job of this remote team is pretty simple: It is to identify ideas that could put you out of business if someone else does them.

SINGLE-PAGE STRATEGIES

According to my friend and entrepreneurial growth guru Verne Harnish, "If you want to get everyone on the same page, you need to get everything literally on one page."

Since I heard him say this in May of 2002 to a room full of startups, Verne has preached the religion of the One-Page Strategic Plan to tens of thousands of business people around the world. Given Verne's background (he has helped create literally dozens of billion-dollar enterprises), it should be no surprise that the idea of aggregating a teams' values, goals, metrics and accountabilities on a single page has become a staple of several successful companies and thought leaders such as Gino Wickman and his entrepreneurial operating system (EOS).

Michael Porter said, "The essence of strategy is choosing what not to do."

And that's the beauty of Verne's idea. It allows (forces, actually) teams to make the toughest decisions quickly and, paraphrasing Verne, leave the room on the same page.

DISRUPTOR TAKEAWAYS AND HACKS

1. **Consistent use of frameworks** allows disruptive leaders to improve their performance over time. The frameworks give them a consistent approach to solve any problem.

2. **"Stumble forward"** is the mantra of the disruptive leader. By getting themselves and their teams into action, they can test, learn and improve ideas. Stumbling forward keeps them from ruining good with perfect.

3. **SMART goals** get teams into action. They don't allow the wiggle room that causes many goals to be suboptimal.

4. **Essential beats important.** Evolved Disruptors have learned how to focus on essential matters now and put important things off until later. They have mastered "diaphoranta."

5. **Choose the higher "yes."** When you are clear on your values, it becomes easier to say "yes" to the right things and in turn say "no" to less valuable opportunities.

Process First, Prize Second

My buddy Jeff Bryk is an entrepreneur who likes to compete. A self-described underdog, he's fought his way into Harvard, onto the trading floor of the Chicago Stock Exchange, and onto the business landscape, starting multiple businesses.

Jeff notes that for many years, he obsessed about his win/loss record; everything was about winning. "Did I win?" "Did I get the promotion?" "What was my finishing time?" "What school did my kid get into?" Then he read: The Score Takes Care of Itself: My Philosophy of Leadership, by the legendary (he won three Super Bowls) coach of the San Francisco 49ers, Bill Walsh.

The book changed everything for Jeff, who immediately began measuring inputs instead of results.

Today, Jeff's advice to his players, friends and clients is to first identify the specific actions and attitudes relevant to your successful performance and production. Once you have done that, concentrate on what will produce results rather than on the results – the process rather than the prize. Paraphrasing Walsh, Jeff believes the results will take care of themselves.

Are you focused on inputs or outputs?

(This space intentionally left empty
so you can doodle.)

Chapter 6
Does It Have To Be A Light Bulb?

I woke up early one Saturday morning and was delighted to see two of my friends talking about business on TV. J.J. Ramberg, host of MSNBC's "Your Business," was chatting with Mike Michalowicz about his latest venture.

What blew me away was that Mike—a wildly creative and outgoing guy—was talking about accounting, one of the most conservative and quiet industries on earth.

I remember thinking, "What in the name of God does Michalowicz know about accounting?"

The answer was pretty simple: Mike knew very little about the business of accounting—which, ironically, explained precisely why he was on TV describing why he was about to disrupt it.

I am going to tell you what Mike was up to in a minute, but first, let me give you some background about him. I'll start here. Even though Mike didn't know a lot about accounting, he knew a tremendous amount about the impact of cash on small businesses. Too many times in the past, he'd felt the pressing weight of poor cash flow as a business owner and had the emotional scars to prove it.

The scars were well earned. As a serial entrepreneur, Mike is not afraid of grabbing the tiger by the tail; and in the process, he created a successful computer network integrations company, a data forensics firm, a (failed) coaching company, and a successful web analytics company. He has also written four books with more on the way, and he produced three TV pilots about entrepreneurship. Not too shabby.

But wait, there's more.

He's also funny—really, really funny. In fact, Mike is the only person who has made me snort beer out of my nose three times in one night. God graciously decided to give Mike a lens that allows him to see the humor, irony and ridiculousness in almost any relationship. His ability to challenge any industry is relevant here because it explains Mike's super-hero talent: He is not just a funny entrepreneur, he is a courageous lateral thinker.

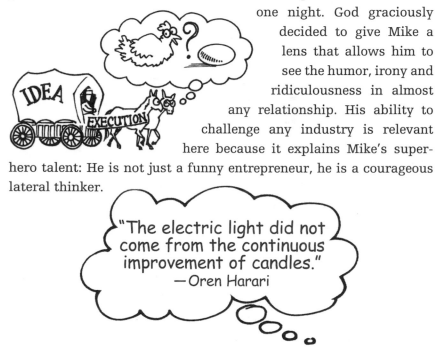

"The electric light did not come from the continuous improvement of candles."
—Oren Harari

Mike starts with "yes," believing there is always a better answer to any challenge. He can objectify, joke about and generate dozens of ideas about how to immediately improve any industry or situation. He can stare down challenges with optimistic eyes wide open. He has very little tolerance for rules or phrases like "that's the way it has always been done." He is fearless when it comes to questioning conventional thinking. He doesn't let little things like his lack of knowledge or experience—or even facts—get in his way while imagining what's next. He trusts his gut, network and tenacity. And he always, ALWAYS believes there is a better way to do…everything.

So in hindsight, I should not have been surprised that Mike had moved on to, of all things, accounting. Why not? He knew almost nothing about the industry. What a perfect place to start if you want to change it.

His latest business is called Profit First, and it's a great example of what happens when you apply lateral thinking (i.e., solving problems by an indirect and creative approach) to something you are curious about.

In this case, Mike started with the question: "Why do business owners pay themselves last?"

Mike had noticed an insidious pattern in himself and other business owners that was resulting in great sacrifice, followed by heavy regret, followed by plummeting mojo, followed by their businesses being shuttered with them having very little to show for it, since they refused to take a salary until all the other bills were paid. Business owners were paying themselves last, despite the fact that they were not only the hardest working but usually the most critical part of their companies.

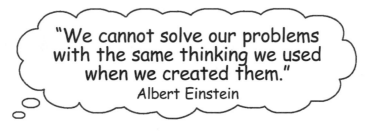

"We cannot solve our problems with the same thinking we used when we created them."
Albert Einstein

Most business owners who are making sure they are the last in line for getting paid can point to some big-hearted and big-brained reasons to explain it away. Reasons like:

- I want to take care of my people first. Or…
- The company needs to be healthy long term. Or…
- My reputation comes before taking a salary. Or….

Mike saw things differently.

His solution is also the title of his book "Profit First: Transform Your Business from a Cash-Eating Monster to a Money-Making Machine."

Mike's theory is that by putting profit first (i.e., literally taking money off the table the moment it comes in the door), business owners would then have to reverse engineer their profitability, spending only what they had left on things like marketing, sales and overhead.

The idea is far from unprecedented. Financial planners always tell us to first save X percent (usually 10 to 20 percent) out of every paycheck and then live on what's left over. But the idea has never been applied to running a business.

This concept is so simple that it is genius. It is also either overlooked or laughed at by professional money managers. But since most small businesses are not run by professional money managers, plain-spoken models like this are refreshingly useful—so useful that Mike built a business around it. He has trained a team of trainers to use his system to help get business owners out of their own way.

All of this was made possible by another fact: Mike thinks like a child. Like other Disruptors, he has maintained the ability to approach challenges like he is still in kindergarten.

KINDERGARTNERS LOVE MARSHMALLOWS

There is a now-famous design challenge that tells us something important about Disruptors. Product designer Peter Skillman and author and futurist Tom Wujec like to talk about this challenge to show how teams approach and succeed—or fail spectacularly—when faced with creative problems.

The marshmallow challenge starts with teams of four people who are asked to build the tallest free-standing structure out of their supplies: 20 sticks of spaghetti, one yard of tape, one yard of string and one marshmallow—that must go on top of the structure.

The challenge is timed, so it forces teams to collaborate very quickly. As you might imagine, this results in a fascinating display of personalities, communication styles, strengths and weaknesses. The exercise not only reveals lessons about how people collaborate under  stress but also the type of person who does best in these situations (hint: people like Mike).

This exercise has taken place hundreds of times, in dozens of countries, and the results are sadly predictable. Out of the gate, executive teams begin to discuss the task. They talk about what the finished tower might look like, they begin to assert their ideas in a way to gain power on the team, they share knowledge, they sketch, they plan, they organize the materials and, finally, they begin to build. Inevitably, just as time is running out, some courageous soul takes the marshmallow and gently attempts to place it on top of the structure while the rest of the team holds their collective breath.

(Anticlimactic music goes here.)

The structure then collapses completely or takes the shape of a post "man-a-pause" phallus, bending sadly toward the disappointed and previously aroused team.[1]

#unhappyending

Perhaps the most fascinating thing about this experiment is the people who consistently deliver the worst results. This list includes recent B-school graduates and lawyers who overanalyze, debate,

---

[1] Sorry, I couldn't resist.

plan and talk their way to towers that are too short or too structurally unsound. On average, only six of 10 teams will actually have structures that are standing at the end of the experiment.

Adding pressure just makes these results worse. Tom Wujec once offered a team of 10 senior executives a $10,000 prize for the tallest structure. At the end of the experiment, exactly zero teams had one that remained erect.[2]

Meanwhile, kindergarten classes consistently outperform executives. Their towers are taller, more creative and more reliable than those of most of the leaders who run companies.

Why?

If you compare and contrast the interactions of the adult teams with the kid teams, you'll see that the children don't waste any oxygen trying to become the leader of the pack. They also don't debate and plan. Instead, they immediately jump in and begin to rapidly experiment.

Trained creative veterans see something else in the behavior of the executives versus the children. The veteran business people are engaged in critical thinking, while the kids are engaged in lateral thinking.

Put simply, critical thinking means dealing with a problem on a straight path toward its most logical solution. In other words, the executives are weighing opinions, arguments and potential solutions against the logical criteria for success. They want to win, so they are using their well-earned experience and knowledge to land on the best and therefore winning solution.

The kids, armed with very little knowledge or experience, engage in lateral thinking. This means they are constantly rearranging a problem to see what new angles may be discovered. It means they are playing with lots of ideas instead of trying to come up with a best one. This type of thinking allows them to delay

---

[2] I know what you're thinking. See? This time I resisted. There is hope.

judgment and maintain an open mind as new options, new angles, new ideas and new solutions present themselves. It creates unexpected "eureka" moments.

The result of these two thinking styles is that while the adults are talking, the kids are prototyping. That means they are getting instant feedback all the way through the process. They are constantly learning what works and what doesn't work while their tower gets taller and taller.

Here are typical marshmallow tower height results according to Tom Wujec:

Average	~20 inches
B-school team	~10 inches
Lawyers	~16 inches
Kindergarten	~27 inches
Architects and engineers	~38 inches[3]
CEOs	~23 inches

So what does this have to do with Disruptors? While interviewing and observing Disruptors, it became apparent that under pressure, they reverted to lateral thinking instead of critical thinking. In other words, just like Mike, they thought like a child.

This is exactly the opposite reaction that most leaders have to pressure. They have been trained to immediately default to planning, logic, past and proven models, and areas of expertise. All of these are fine in moderation, but if they are your only go-to punch, just like in the marshmallow experiment, this reflex will often get organizations more stuck than unstuck.

We all need more eureka moments. And these moments almost always come from lateral thinking like Mike Michalowicz's conclusion that business owners should make taking profits the first thing they do.

---

[3] Knowledge helps here. According to Tom, "They understand that triangles and self-reinforcing geometrical patterns are the key to building stable structures."

MOVING FROM CRITICAL TO LATERAL

Years ago, I was sitting in a meeting with my friend and co-worker Joe Kim when he came up with yet another unexpected and brilliant idea. This caused me to say, "Man, you are an Idea Monkey, Joe. You're naturally good at coming up with unexpected ideas."

Joe immediately disagreed.

"Thanks, but I am actually naturally terrible at coming up with ideas. I was so bad that I had to train myself to use a couple of frameworks to appear more creative than I actually am."

I was stunned. I had no idea that what appeared to be spontaneity was Joe working through a framework.

It turns out that, as Joe discovered, leaders and teams can use simple frameworks to shift from critical thinking to lateral thinking. We talked about frameworks in the last chapter, but I deliberately left the following three out so we could talk about them here.

So if you consider yourself a professional who leans to conservative and proven methods under pressure, here are three useful ways to think more expansively about a problem.

SCAMPER

Imagine you and your team are staring at a challenge, and all of your solutions seem to be uninspired. Welcome to the world of critical thinking. You simply know too much to be creative.

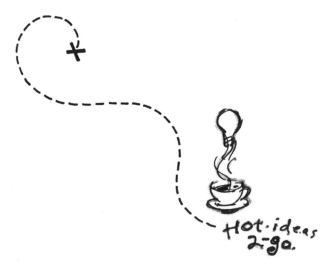

Hot·ideas 2-go.

At times like these, it may be time to SCAMPER. SCAMPER is an acronym that stands for:

S ubstitute	What or who could you use instead?
C ombine	What could we combine or bring together?
A dapt	What could be adapted for use as a solution?
M odify	Can we change the item in some way?
P ut to other uses	What new ways could this be used?
E liminate	What can we get rid of?
R earrange	What could we change around?

Here's an example. Your team is working on developing new products, services or business models to solve for this insight:

I like having insurance because I feel protected, but the process for getting it is too complicated.

Your teams' so-so solution to this problem: educate and train insurance agents to make the experience of buying insurance value-added and more consultative.

There is nothing wrong with what you have come up with, but no one thinks it comes anywhere near a breakthrough. It is a classic product of critical thinking.

Now let's use SCAMPER to force some lateral thinking.

S ubstitute	We could replace the application process with online games like "RealAge" that exchange personal information for fun results or prizes.
C ombine	You signed up for a triathlon or executive annual physical? Great! You automatically qualify for an insurance product.
A dapt	Could we use artificial intelligence that helps identify certain segments to waive application steps?
M odify	Can we "protect" new things that people care about (e.g., their data, pictures, pets or iPhones)?
P ut to other uses	Could our agents be redeployed to sell other complicated products (e.g., in-home health care)?
E liminate	Why do I need to talk to someone? Can we design a way for people to buy products direct online?
R earrange	Can we offer products with no application process first and modified policies second?

WW__D?

My friend and co-worker Brett Miller likes to tell the story about a day he was driving to work, thinking about a tough challenge. He was stuck in traffic behind a car with a *What Would Jesus? Do* bumper sticker. Brett found himself asking exactly that: What WOULD Jesus do about this particular challenge he was trying to figure out? Which led him to another series of questions:

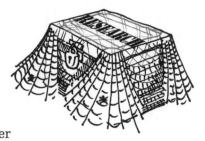

What would Steve Jobs do?
What would Oprah do?
What would Mark Zuckerberg do?
What would Melinda Gates do?
What would Elon Musk do?

When we force ourselves to see a challenge through the lens of an inventor, entrepreneur, luminary or visionary, we can readily think more laterally. As a result, we can get dramatically different and more disruptive ideas.

For example, let's go back to that insurance challenge we were wrestling with. Mark Zuckerberg might turn insurance into a crowd-funding platform, where a large pool of friends pitches in to protect people in their group. That's right, that high school reunion group just became a way to buy cheaper insurance together.

> "If you believe you can or believe you can't, you're right."
> — Henry Ford

Think about it. Zuckerberg could actually do this, as my partner Maria Ferrante-Schepis wrote in the *Huffington Post*. After all, Facebook represents a giant pool of people that has qualitative and quantitative data about lifestyle, age, habits and peer groups.

Besides, who better to insure your future than your friends? If this idea seems farfetched, remember that it is basically how insurance first got started. People in small communities would pass the hat to take care of those in need.

WIN POWERBALL

There is a great Steve Martin bit titled "You Can Be a Millionaire (and never pay taxes)." Mr. Martin starts it like this: "You say, Steve, how can I be a millionaire and never pay taxes? First, get a million dollars."

Imagine what you would do if you had $1 million. Now imagine what you would do if you had $100 million. Most of us would agree, there isn't much that we couldn't do if we had $100 million. The possibilities are virtually endless!

So (hypothetically) give your team or yourself $100 million. Imagine how you would approach that difficult challenge you are facing if you had unlimited funds. Too often we employ critical thinking because we are so aware of the financial constraints related to a challenge. Removing the constraints allows us to think laterally just for a moment.

An axiom of innovation and Disruptors is that it is impossible to make a small idea big, but it is easy to make a big idea small. Start with a big, $100 million idea, then go to work on how to make the essence of the idea a reality, regardless of the budget.

Here's a $100 Million Example

I am frustrated when I go on executive retreats. I'd like to take teams to a vacation resort town where my family has a home. But since the family home is a cottage with a single bathroom and only two beds, there isn't enough room to have meetings. This leaves only a few options, and we usually rent multiple hotel rooms and find a beige, boring conference room for our meetings. So much for meeting at a beautiful lake retreat.

What if I had $1 million? I would build an executive retreat with 15 rooms, a beautiful meeting area, a bar, a game room and walking trails.

Here's the thing: I could get a loan and do this today. It would then be a cash flowing property—instead of a little cottage—that would be a place for my family and business teams from around the country to meet.

Maybe I should visit a bank.

DON'T WAIT TO INNOVATE

Here is a fact that the best leaders understand but everyone else wrestles with: Innovation needs to be countercyclical. In order to allow your teams the oxygen they require to engage in lateral thinking, the best time to create the "next big thing" is when things are going well, not when you are struggling.

When the economy is booming and their company is crushing it in the marketplace, most leaders tend to reap the benefits. As the saying goes, they make hay while the sun shines.

But then the rain comes. Or the economy slows. Or your once-reliable products or services become stale. Or there are unexpected new competitors. Or people are buying direct. Or…. You know the list.

As a result, the phone stops ringing and your sales department starts to clamor for new things to sell.

Only then does leadership spring into action, assembling their brightest, most creative people to chart a new course, fueled by inspired thinking and new offerings.

But by this point, it is too late and the marshmallow experiment points to a key reason why.

Unfortunately, as I mentioned in the last chapter, your company is perfectly engineered to create the outcomes it is creating. In other words, it knows how to do the same thing it did yesterday, *juuuuuust* a little better today. It also knows how to kill anything that doesn't resemble what you did yesterday. Your company is filled with experts who have been trained to think critically—not laterally—about challenges.

So under the pressure of slowing sales or waning market relevance, your perfectly engineered machine will tighten its grip on the past. The well-meaning team members will focus relentlessly on your core business (their past success formula) thus accelerating your demise because what worked in the past will no longer work in the future. Making a better buggy whip, a faster film camera, a quieter typewriter or even cleaner coal won't keep the stagecoach operators, film processors, typewriter manufacturers or miners employed.

You need a different plan, which means you need a different kind of thinking—lateral thinking. And for most teams, this is only possible to achieve when your CFO is smiling.

The lesson is pretty simple: Make sure you are thinking about what's next when your current offering is doing well; plant seeds while you are harvesting.

DISRUPTOR TAKEAWAYS AND HACKS

Here are three proven ways to help your team start with "yes" and think more expansively when faced with a challenge.

1. **Import new thinking.** My favorite saying is: "You can't read the label when you are sitting inside the jar." Simply put, the longer you are working on a challenge, project, relationship... the more your expertise keeps you from seeing new possibilities. Nothing changes this reality faster than bringing in new leadership from outside your company and, even better, your industry. It is easier for people outside the jar to think laterally.

2. **Start over.** If you had to start over and recreate your company or a product or service from scratch, what would it look like? What business model would you use? What technology would you employ? Would you sell it direct or through channel partners? Would you sell a different mix of products and services? Remember, the upstart entrepreneur is not limited by your current operating model, paradigms or people. (Just think about Mike Michalowicz and his approach to accounting.) If you can take a truly fresh look at your industry, you might just be able to disrupt yourself.

DISRUPTOR TAKEAWAYS AND HACKS (cont.)

But if you can't...

3. Outsource your crazy. There is a paradox when it comes to innovation. It sounds like this: "We need to think more like entrepreneurs, but those people are crazy!" After years of seeing leaders reach for revolutionary innovation while their teams desperately try to appease current clients, leadership and budgets, I have landed on a simple truth: Evolution happens inside your walls and revolution happens outside. Want to start a revolution? Invest in companies that will someday disrupt you. Meanwhile, let your people get better and better at evolutionary, incremental wins.

Your brilliant, insightful, amusing,
life-changing notes go here.
Also useful for wrapping small fish.

Chapter 7
Embrace The **Hate To Innovate**

Ron Repking was losing his mind. His complaints were getting louder and louder, but he wasn't being listened to and he was beginning to feel helpless.

Ron hated feeling helpless.

I had known Ron for years, and his reputation as an extremely successful, even-tempered entrepreneur was well earned. But as I listened to him on the phone, he was as worked up as I had ever heard him.

"Mike, I am so sorry for recommending that school for your son, Gunnar. It's an absolute train wreck. It's a clown show over there—and they aren't responding to the suggestions Liz (Ron's wife) and I keep making."

I, of course, was oblivious to what Ron was talking about. As new parents, Ruthie and I were too busy trying to figure out how to avoid screwing up our first child to understand what Ron was seeing at the school our son attended (on Ron's recommendation).[1]

Ruthie and I had moved into our town because of its great public schools. But as new-to-the-area parents, we had no idea how com-

---

[1] Of course, we totally screwed up our kids. Just ask them.

petitive it was to get a child into preschool—seriously, PRESCHOOL. By the time we figured it out, there was a ridiculously long waiting list everywhere. Thank God our friend Ron was able to pull some strings and get our kid into the local Montessori school his son attended.

But now, incredibly, Ron was on the phone apologizing for the favor.

"I hate how they are teaching our kids. I hate how disorganized they are. I hate that the classrooms are a mess. I hate the chaos and  that they are not controlling the troublemakers. I hate that we're paying for school and getting subpar day care. I hate that my son isn't learning anything anymore. I hate that he doesn't like the experience. Like I said, I am so sorry I got you guys into this mess."

Huh?

As far as Ruth and I were concerned, the school was fine, and our son was having a great time. But the fact that Ron was telling us that it was a disaster now had me a little concerned. Despite my family's gene pool, I figured our son was destined to play quarterback for Harvard. We couldn't have a bad preschool experience ruin that outcome.

So Ruthie and I began to track Ron's campaign to improve things.

After countless meetings with the principal of the school, during which he was told that education was complicated, he did not understand how kids learned, he was not an expert (they were), other parents were not concerned (probably talking about us), things would get better, and it is really, really hard to run a school....

Ron decided he was tired of listening to himself complain. Like I said, Ron hated feeling helpless.

You probably see where this story is going.

Later that year, Ron and Liz started their own school, taking their two favorite teachers and a handful of the kids who were attending the Montessori—including our son and their son—with them. Today, their school is thriving. More important, while none of its students have ended up playing quarterback at Harvard, many went on to attend fine colleges and had impressive academic careers.

Ron's example shows us how Disruptors move quickly from hate to ideas to action to creating products, services and experiences that we love to love.

EMBRACE THE HATE

Imagine you're speed dating. You move from table to table looking for someone who will "get" your magical mojo. You describe yourself this way: "I like long walks on the beach, listening to '80s arena rock, any movie by John Hughes, dogs, barbecuing, biking, fishing, traveling, wine, and, oh yeah, I absolutely love camping, like carry-your-own-toilet-paper camping."

When you finally find your match, you want to spend every moment with your new soul mate. Their opinion now matters most to you. After all, they tell you that they're your biggest fan, and they are willing to go with you to a Styx concert one day and off the grid the next. (Sigh.) Life is good.

Most of us like to be liked, and that (according to Barry Calpino, former head of innovation for Kraft) poses an often overlooked opportunity for innovators.

Calpino (a legendary corporate Disruptor) argues that when we constantly look to our most loyal customers and fans for feedback and insights, we miss the opportunity to hear about the glaring gaps in our performance.

While your No. 1 fan tells you *what* you want to hear, haters will tell you what you *need* to hear.

REALLY IMPORTANT: The order here matters. Start with the Insight, then have an Idea.

It turns out that the people you passed up in our speed dating metaphor have the most to offer you in terms of game-changing feedback. Says Calpino, "If you occasionally go to the people who absolutely loathe your product or service and ask them for feedback, you'll often find HUGE opportunities to improve your offering."

> Once you start looking at mature industries, you will see that hate is everywhere. For Disruptors inside and outside your organization, there is no better opportunity.

His advice is simple: Embrace the haters. In a dating scenario, you might get by without doing it. After all, you are only looking for THE ONE. But in business, unless you are planning on being an extremely small niche product, you need to expand your horizons.

One Simple Place to Find Opportunities

Wherever there are experts and a complicated purchasing process, opportunity abounds to learn from haters. Let's look at just one example: health care.

Show of hands...who hates going to hospitals; getting eight "this is not a bill" statements for every medical procedure; the fact that doctors make you wait...and wait and never apologize; those drafty gowns that reveal your butt; having to answer the same questions every time you show up at the office; getting put on hold when you call in and having to answer the same questions every time you get transferred; the "Is this covered?" insurance vortex...? You get the idea.

The point is that those who hate what you are providing in the health care field are doing everything short of begging for a better alternative—BEGGING. This means that someone who can deliver that better solution will steal away your customers as soon as they do.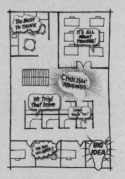

The message for you is simple: If you ignore the haters, you are ignoring your biggest Achilles' heel. If you listen to the haters, you'll hear that opportunity abounds.

Disruptors become famous because of a simple fact: They embrace the hate to innovate.

Disruptors who embrace the hate—and the best of them do—will point you to new products, services and business models that your loyal customers would never consider. (Why should they? They are perfectly happy!)

For example, true environmentalists probably don't drive V8 trucks that guzzle gas, but they certainly could help transportation companies think up ideas that would lead them in the direction of sustainable fuels, fractional ownership of vehicles, worksharing of heavy vehicles and the like.

Calpino notes that soup haters complained about thin soup and thus Chunky soup was born. Ziploc containers were born directly from his former team listening to complaints about Tupperware and Rubbermaid. Since Barry was a Disruptor himself, he was happy to hear the complaints and take action.

Disruptors, armed with hate and the creator's mindset, have produced thousands of products that we all love. I believe listening to the haters helped invent the Roomba, deodorant, air freshener, mouthwash, SnapChat, Amazon Prime, DVRs, and the prenuptial agreement. In response to hate, these products eliminated chores, smells, embarrassing photos, waiting, videotapes and the ginormous legal fees associated with divorce.

YOU CAN DO THIS INTERNALLY

This same kind of thinking also works inside your company. For example, if you lead a life insurance team, instead of going to your No. 1 salesperson for new ideas (you know, the one you just gave the giant commission check to), why not talk to the young new hire who shows incredible promise but can't sell anything to save her own life?

Why is this commissionless person beginning to hate you and the company? It may just be that her peers—the people she is trying to sell to—are no longer interested in what you have to sell. That's right. Millennials might not be into annuities or whole life policies. Maybe she can help you create new products and get a large commission check at the same time. When she does, you will have turned a hater into a lover, creating more profits in the process.

Question: Who knew this could be possible in the insurance industry?

Answer: The haters knew, but the industry forgot to ask them. This is one reason why there is now a $15 trillion insurance gap according to a study by LIMRA, the Life Insurance and Market Research Association. It is also why a total of $3.8 billion was invested in the category in 2016 and 2017 by upstarts  bent on disrupting the industry. Investors saw all the hate and wondered why nobody had done something about it.

WHY WE DON'T FEEL THE HEAT (OR THE HATE)

A few years ago, I invited Richard and Linda Eyre to coach a group of entrepreneurs about parenting. The Eyres, who have written a number of books, are experts on the topic, and as an earnestly struggling parent myself, I loved hearing their perspective, their stories and their wisdom.

Their ideas were simple and compelling. One parenting technique involved using visual metaphors to heighten a child's awareness and teach them what they should value. For example, they suggested telling kids a story about what happens to crabs in a pot of water on a stove.

As the water gets hotter, one crab may try to climb out, only to be pulled back into the water by another. The lesson here is to be careful who you are hanging out with. The wrong people will continually pull you into hot water, and everyone winds up getting cooked. Again, I will quote UCLA Hall of Fame basketball coach John Wooden who said, "Show me your friends and I'll show you your future."

Today, when Ruthie and I sense our kids are hanging with the wrong crowd, we simply say one word: "crabs." They immediately get the metaphor—and the message.

A similar metaphor sticks with me because it reminds me why we can't hear the haters. This metaphor, which you may have heard in a different context, has to do with frogs.

Editors note: My apologies to frog lovers. I, too, love frogs. Trying to catch and release those slippery buggers brings back great memories from my childhood. Today, nothing says "great ecosystem" better than the sounds of frogs at dusk. So please don't try the following at home.

Think back to the crab story. Imagine the same stove and the same pot of water, only this time the water is nice and cool and full of frogs. "Things are great," think the frogs as they lounge in the cool waters of their successful industry, the pot in our metaphor. "We're swimming in profits!"

Only things aren't so great. The flames of competition are slowly heating up the water. Amazon, Google and a zillion startups have all been firing up new products aimed at the industry. But because the temperature is rising at a steady, almost undetectable rate, the indicators go unnoticed or are ignored. In fact, the frogs that have been in the pot for a while—sometimes decades—insist things are just fine. "Our clients love us! Just wait things out until they get back to normal," they tell each other.

If you're watching this story unfold, you may be screaming to the frogs that they are in trouble, but they just don't agree. They just sit there and do nothing.

We know how this story ends. The frogs get cooked, along with their shareholders and employees.

Ironically, if you tossed a new frog into the water as it was heating up, it would jump out. It would immediately know that things weren't right and that something had to change. It would scream complaints. It would be a hater. You would likely call this frog a Disruptor.

And herein lies the lesson: It is almost always the newest frog in the pot that feels the heat and jumps into action, responding to the changes in the marketplace.

So if your CEO, senior managers or people who work for you seem to be enjoying a few too many hot tubs, it's time to bring in some new frogs—some Disruptors—or get out of the water before it's too late.

Riiiiiiibbit.

BEING HATED IS HARD; HERE'S WHAT TO DO ABOUT IT

Disruptors know that there is a simple question that, when deeply considered, can change your business in an instant.

It is a question that enormous companies usually get wrong and small companies often get right—simply because the small company was usually started by a Disruptor.

It is a question central to many of the world's most profound innovations.

The question is this: "What business am I really in?"

This is a great question to ask when your legacy products or services are falling out of favor when you are starting to feel less love and more hate.

If you answer the question "What business am I really in?" too quickly, or you are a leader of a historically successful company or industry, you probably just answered wrong.

I'll explain.

Harvard Business School professor Theodore Levitt, back in 1960, captured one of the major challenges most companies face today. His now classic article "Marketing Myopia" begins this way:

> "Every major industry was once a growth industry. But some that are now riding a wave of growth enthusiasm are very much in the shadow of decline. Others, which are thought of as seasoned growth industries, have actually stopped growing. In every case, the reason growth is threatened, slowed, or stopped is not [emphasis in the original] because the market is saturated. It is because there has been a failure of management."

This failure is caused by what Levitt called "marketing myopia," which he defines exactly as you would expect. It's what happens when company leaders define their mission too narrowly. In other words, it's a form of business nearsightedness or shortsightedness.

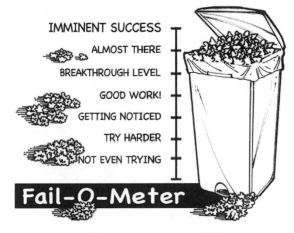

As you might have guessed, marketing myopia helps us see love and keeps us from seeing hate.

I spoke to author and thought leader Clayton Christensen about this concept. He frames it this way: You need to ask, "What is the job to be done?" For example, Clayton says that the owner of a drill bit company will say, "We are in the drill bit-making business." This answer is the result of marketing myopia. Clayton would argue that the owner is in the hole-making business.

Levitt would have been proud. He used to say that no one went to the hardware store (which we would update today to include Lowe's and The Home Depot) to buy a drill. They went there to buy a quarter-inch hole.

Marketing myopia results in most seasoned executives asking questions that are indeed important but limiting. Their questions typically are about cutting costs, how to beat the competition by selling more, and what improvements to make to the legacy products and services that customers have always loved. Since their well-established competitors are asking the same questions, the result is a race to the bottom, thanks to shrinking margins (due to the increased competition) and a smaller customer base, as people continue looking for things that are new and better.

And even if they (and unfortunately the "they" often includes you and me) can bring themselves to ask a seemingly obvious question like "What business are we in?" they are too used to doing what they have always done and thinking the way they always have to muster a novel perspective. Using Levitt's language, we've become myopic.

Levitt offered what are now a few classic examples:

INDUSTRY	MYOPIC PURPOSE	THE BROADER PURPOSE
Railroads	Train travel	Transportation
Hollywood	Movies	Entertainment
Oil companies	Petroleum	Energy

To that list, we could add Clayton Christensen's example:

INDUSTRY	MYOPIC PURPOSE	THE BROADER PURPOSE
Tools	Drill bits	Hole making

Here are a few more related examples worthy of consideration because they represent important industries that are under pressure and are missing obvious opportunities to innovate:

INDUSTRY	MYOPIC PURPOSE	THE BROADER PURPOSE
Hospitals	Treating the sick	
Health insurers	Medical costs	
Schools	Education	
Lawyers	Practicing law	

I left the broader purpose lines blank to make a simple point: If you are not in the hospital or health insurance business, or in the education or legal industry, you are more likely to see great possibility here. After all, for you as

an outsider, there is no risk in suggesting an idea that runs contrary to the existing business model. It is even easier to do if you've had experiences you have hated with any of the categories above.

If you were able to fill in the third column, congratulations. You are now seeing things like a Disruptor.

So some 50 years after Professor Levitt wrote his article, what's our takeaway? I think it boils down to this: We must stop thinking about what we sell to lovers and think more about what we are NOT selling to haters, and figure out how we can get those haters to buy.

For example:

- Who are the people we can help?
- Which assets at our disposal are currently underutilized?
- What do these people REALLY need that can be provided by us?
- Are we ticking them off? When, how and why?
- Could any of the answers to the questions above lead us to a new product, service or business?
- What would we look like if we started our company from scratch today?

Let's use a simple example that came from my colleague Maria Ferrante-Schepis. She spent the first half of her career working in insurance, an industry that told itself that it was in the protection business. This makes perfect sense.

But insurance companies, when you really think about it, are not just in the protection business. They are in the "lifestyle continuity business"—keeping the lives of individuals, businesses and families intact when the unexpected happens.

Naturally, different types of people have different lifestyles. It is when you fail to understand the type of lifestyle that someone wants, which is glaringly apparent when you offer them a mismatched product offering, that you begin to see hate—lots and lots of hate.

Using Maria's example, we can see that by simply broadening the business definition, it helps companies in the insurance industry potentially expand beyond what is offered today, to create new possibilities and innovations for the future, and to hear from and alter their offering in response to the haters.

So what possibilities open up for the insurance industry? Here's an example that your grandfather would have laughed at 30 years ago: protecting the lifestyles of pets.

Today, boomers and millennials are humanizing their pets. They are treating their pets like their parents and grandparents used to treat their kids. And the amount of disposable income spent on pets, everything from toys to health care, is mind-boggling. Spending in this category, which has been climbing at double-digit rates in recent years, is now estimated at $70 billion annually just in the U.S.

Since people are seeing their pets as part of the family, they naturally hate it when insurance companies don't see things the same way.

"Honey, I think we're gonna need a different trap."

Seeing things as the market does, as opposed to seeing things the way you always have, is why you read that CVS is buying Aetna. It is in response to a need to make providing health care simpler—and Walmart is pursuing Humana. (Can you imagine getting an annual physical and filling all of your prescriptions at your local Walmart?) It is how IBM transformed from manufacturing computers to an IT and computer services company. It is how Nintendo went from being a playing card company to a video game powerhouse. It is how Western Union transformed from a telegraph company to a money transfer company. It is how Apple got in the PC, phone and music business.

The companies that are best at constantly asking "What business are we really in?" are the hardest ones to categorize. For example, what business is Google really in?[2]

GOOGLE: THE ANTIDOTE TO MYOPIA AND HATERS

Speaking of Google, there is a simple way to cure marketing myopia and, in the process, understand how others are finding and dealing with their haters. You simply examine the benefits (instead of the products or services) you deliver to your customers.

For example, you may say you are in the informed solutions, education providing, qualified options, quick research, packaged choices, thought leadership business. If you are, you are in good company. When you Google these words, you'll find that, as defined by benefits delivered, you're in the same business as Blue Cross Blue Shield, Orbitz, Amazon, Angie's List, WebMD and Edmunds.com.

Now, what could you learn from leaders in these businesses about innovative products and services? What did their customers once hate about them? How did they respond?

We've used this process to find experts in parallel industries solving the same types of problems we are working on. And it helps our clients to think objectively and parallel engineer ideas. That's the politically correct way Disruptors describe "stealing" ideas (i.e., taking an idea that someone else developed and improving upon it).

So it turns out that the simple question "What business are we really in?" can provide the growth answers you are seeking.

---

[2] The defense rests.

When you are able to take a fresh, consumer-driven look at the business you are in, it creates a world of new possibilities to innovate.

The reason this is important is simple. Change matters. Academics have shown that 54 percent of a company's stock price is based on ideas that company leaders haven't even thought about yet. In other words, investors are betting on your ability to respond to changing market conditions and innovate.

For you more spiritual readers, the Dalai Lama once said that the greatest gift we could give our children is to prepare them for great change. Indeed, with information doubling yearly, and technology granting data access and opportunity to billions of new people, change is upon us. And it is coming faster and faster.

THE AMOUNT OF A STOCK'S VALUE TIED TO THE FUTURE *

* HARVARD BUSINESS REVIEW

ARE WE ABOUT TO BE DISRUPTED?

Yes, disruption can even happen to you. There comes a time in every business when it becomes apparent that your product, service or business model is no longer relevant. The following symptoms are clues that the shift is about to hit the fan. Why? Because Disruptors in your industry will examine each of these symptoms and attack the underlying hate driving them. The nine symptoms:

1. **Great consolidation is afoot.** Your competitors are joining forces. You are becoming a smaller fish in a bigger pond. You may be asking yourself, "How can I possibly compete with the big boys if they keep getting bigger and bigger?"

2. **You don't recognize your competitors anymore.** There are companies entering your space, but they look completely different than you. They have new ways of making money, selling, distributing…. They are breaking rules that your people are telling you are sacred and unbreakable. And, worse, these upstarts are making substantial sums while doing it.

3. **The competitive pressures on your business are increasing dramatically.** Pressure could be a synonym for lower price, but it also could mean customer demands, speed-to-market complaints, and product or service customization requests. You are being asked why you can't deliver the same levels of delight that the new kid on the block can.

4. **Simple solutions are not enough to make people happy.** Your customers are demanding higher and higher levels of product complexity.

5. **Technology is replacing people.** Tasks, which years ago seemed complex, are now being done automatically.

6. **Some customers are getting all the attention.** You notice that more and more of your competitors are trying to serve only the best customers. Uh-oh. Those are the 20 percent that drive 80 percent of your margins.

7. **Part of the market is being left behind.** In an effort to follow the margins and money, there is a growing segment of the market that is being neglected.

8. **You are losing your power to manage the supply and distribution of your product or service.** For example, if the manufacturer decides to sell direct, where does that leave everyone else in the distribution chain?

9. **It is getting more complicated to do what you do.** Perhaps regulations are increasing, or there just seem to be more process hoops to jump through to serve your customer.

At this point, asking if these symptoms sound familiar would be rhetorical. Virtually every industry, including the "untouchables" like higher education, health care, legal services, strategy consulting and investment banking, are now battling Disruptors and disruption.

Have you seen *OUR* idea?

AVOIDING THE NAPSTER MOMENT

There are three critical steps to take to make sure you don't experience a Napster Moment—that extremely specific point in time we talked about at the beginning of the book—when someone with no business being in your business comes along and puts you out of business.

Step 1: Get ridiculously close to your customer's customer's customer. Do NOT leave it up to distribution partners or traditional industry experts to see the future needs of the end consumer. They sell to lovers, not haters. You must discover the hate and the resulting opportunities for yourself. You must hear directly from the consumers that your product, service or business model was intended to delight—but now is infuriating. The company that has the deepest intimacy with the end customer has an unfair competitive advantage when it comes to what's next. While they are playing the B2B or B2C game, you have to be thinking B2 "me."

True innovation starts with the end consumer. Here's the punch line: We've entered the B2Me age. The companies that are best at listening to and understanding the changing needs of their consumers and responding with new products and services will outlast, outearn and outperform their B2B (business-to-business) rivals. They know that if they rely on their channel partners or inside experts for insight, they will soon be extinct.

Step 2: Be agnostic. The end consumer wants something from you that you are not providing; that's why they are mad. Forget thinking about the business you are in today and let their wishes drive the business you COULD be in tomorrow. As I mentioned earlier, the one thing the most innovative companies have in common is that they think expansively about who they serve and how they may serve them. For example, what business is Apple in? Computers? Phones? Music? Money?[3]

Step 3: Make sure you have identified and deeply understand a segment—and a significant need that segment has—before you begin creating unique solutions. Remember the pet insurance example. Your customers are consumers who are saying, "Please understand me."

A caveat: If your company is full of imaginative people with an entrepreneurial mindset, you will likely jump to many solutions before you do the hard work of finding the right segment and the right itch to scratch. That would be a mistake. You must strive for deep understanding first, ideas second.

> **Monkey Fact: Ideas are easy**
>
> Only one out of 5,000 "big ideas" see commercial success.

On the other hand, if you've built a team that believes in operational rigor, you'll likely focus on unimaginative ideas that always seemed to work with past customers. This is an even bigger mistake—one that signals the end of your business. You have turned a deaf ear to the haters, and there are not enough lovers left to sustain the business.

The last point may seem like common sense, yet some of the most intelligent leaders make the mistake all the time.

---

[3] The defense rests (again).

LOVE AND HATE: A LESSON FROM FOX NEWS AND MSNBC

I now know that Facebook secretly tagged me as a moderate, so at least to artificial intelligence, I have a balanced political view. To make sure this remains true, I've spent quite a bit of time on sites like PolitiFact.com and Snopes just to make sure I wasn't imagining something that everyone else knows is true: The right and the left find ways to love and hate the exact opposite points of view.

So if you really want a "fair and balanced" look at political issues, try quickly switching back and forth between FOX and MSNBC. Three things will happen:

1. You'll hear dramatically different perspectives on just about everything.
2. You'll end up being confused.
3. You'll understand that your favorite politicians, journalists and commentators can teach you something about innovation—specifically, how not to be innovative.

This polarity became stunningly clear years ago when a GOP-led panel released their Benghazi probe findings in 2016. According to CBS news, the bipartisan panel concluded:

> "The CIA and the military acted properly in responding to the 2012 attack on a U.S. diplomatic compound in Benghazi, Libya."

The report asserted no wrongdoing by Obama administration officials. None.

This report ran in the face of a then long-standing quote on Sean Hannity's website:

> "The Obama administration has gone to great lengths to lie and manipulate the truth regarding what really happened almost two years ago when our consulate was attacked in Benghazi and four brave Americans were killed."

Mr. Hannity was not alone in his view on FOX. Since that terrible event in Benghazi on September 11, 2012, FOX personalities, in what could be described as perspective judo, creatively found ways to fan a flame that, as the Congressional report concluded, should have gone out of their own accord.

To be clear, I am not picking on FOX. You don't have to be a high-strung conservative to deliver "unfair and unbalanced" perspectives. When it comes to looking through a tilted lens, we're all quite capable, regardless of our political affiliation or industry.

For example, in 2010 on ABC's "This Week," Bill Maher, speaking on behalf of "the left," shared what he thought was a fact but turned out to be an opinion when he said, "I mean, Brazil got off oil in the last 30 years; we certainly could have." Missing in Mr. Maher's perspective is that Brazil is actually the sixth largest global consumer of oil at over 3 million barrels A DAY.

Rachel Maddow, perhaps MSNBC's biggest star, has been accused of the same type of distorted perspective: "Despite what you may have heard about Wisconsin's finances," she said back in 2016, "Wisconsin is on track to have a budget surplus this year—I'm not kidding."

"You can't read the label when you are sitting inside the jar."

She may not be kidding, but after hearing her say these words, I checked. According to the Associated Press, *The Milwaukee Journal Sentinel* and Wisconsin's governor, the state was projecting a deficit of between $78 million and $340 million. Maddow relied on a memo prepared by Robert Lang, the director of the nonpartisan Legislative Fiscal Bureau. But a quick review of the fine print of his report showed a $137 million shortfall.

Researchers will tell you that you can make numbers tell almost any story if you have a story you want to tell. You just have to be creative.

Now, "creative interpretation" of facts is nothing new, of course. What is new is that we are becoming deaf to facts or opinions that do not support our own beliefs. These have become "alternative facts" or "fake news" no matter which side of the political aisle you are on.

So what does all this have to do with Disruptors you ask? The answer is simple: The best ones avoid confirmation bias. Too many experts look for evidence that their opinion of how a problem should be solved is correct. In doing so, they sacrifice the opportunity to be curious and learn about possibilities.

When was the last time you were willing to hear dramatically different perspectives at work? Or when was the last time you went looking for them outside your industry? Most of us don't have the systems, culture or leadership in place to get fair and balanced feedback. If we aren't willing to learn—and instead spend all our time trying to prove why we are right—eventually we put ourselves out of business. People and companies that know how to get truly fair and balanced perspectives eat our lunch.

So the next time you hear a professor, a lawyer, a doctor, an agent, a store manager, etc., cite a "fact" about higher education, practicing law, medicine, insurance, or the state of retail today or in the future, remember these fine words from Mark Twain:

> "It ain't what you don't know that gets you in trouble. It's what you know for sure that just ain't so." — Mark Twain

INSIGHT FIRST, IDEA SECOND

Over a decade ago, when people still put film in cameras, our company worked with Kodak. At the time, there were other companies getting into the film business. When asked about the new competitors, Kodak's most senior R&D leader assured us they were not competitors at all. Kodak's film, paper and chemicals were so superior, he said, that he did not see the new entrants as a threat. He was correct...sort of. Kodak had spent decades perfecting accurate imaging, and they were the undisputed leader in quality.

Unfortunately for Kodak, Fuji had entered the market with a product that was cheaper—one that created brighter, more colorful pictures. While the experts agreed that Fuji's product was photographically inaccurate, many consumers and customers liked it better. A giant retailer put the new competitive film on the shelf, and people bought it. Kodak never saw it coming because they were so convinced of their position.

My friend Jeffrey Hazlett eventually became Kodak's CMO. Jeffrey is an entrepreneur and a Disruptor. When I shared this story with him, he scoffed and said that despite what I heard from the "experts" at Kodak, Fuji entering the market was the tipping point for the company. Obviously, this was not the Kodak Moment management was looking for at the time.

Confirmation bias and expertise can get in the way. We may be so convinced that our technology or business model is better that we misjudge what our customers are willing to buy. Many of the same experts who argued for Kodak's film superiority also argued that consumers would never accept digital imaging. This is exactly what expertise and confirmation bias look like.

And no industry is immune.

For years:

- Professors argued against online learning, saying it would never catch on.
- Banks argued against digital currency. "Just a fad," bankers said.
- Doctors argued against urgent care clinics in Walmart and the Minute Clinics at CVS. "Who would get their medical care that way?"
- Retailers argued against online purchasing. "People love shopping, and they need to see and feel the merchandise."
- Financial advisors argued against artificial intelligence that could provide advice, what we now call robo-advisors. "Who wants their financial advice from a machine?"
- Big oil argued against alternative energy like solar and wind. "It's not practical and never will be."

What do you — someone who is an expert — argue against? When we start with our biases (e.g., there will always be film, hospitals, cash, universities and coal mines…), innovation fails us.

So how should hate impact the way we think about innovation? Innovation occurs when you combine:

1. A significant unmet need or insight (the bigger the hate, the bigger the insight) with
2. A product, service or business model that meets that need (makes them love you, not hate you) and
3. There is clear communication or an experience that links No. 1 to No. 2.

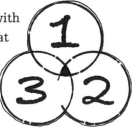

Insight

Communication/ Experience

Idea

1970s rock icon Meat Loaf sang "Two Out of Three Ain't Bad," but even though I am a sucker for arena rock, I respectfully disagree. Without all three of these things (the idea, the insight and the communication that links and explains the two) in perfect alignment, the innovation will fail.[4]

To change the world, you need to create the synchronized intersection—the tiny center area within the three circles above.

That's hard!

This simple formula is easy to describe but perilously difficult to achieve. It turns out that ideas are easy, insights are easy and communication is easy. Getting them all to work in unison? That's really, really hard—and it's why most new products fail.

To use another metaphor, think of the diagram above as a three-legged stool. Without one leg, the stool falls over—and so, too, will your innovation initiative or entrepreneurial venture. You may have a great team of brilliant idea people (Idea Monkeys), but unless you can get them to understand this simple concept, they will fail. Your job as the lord of the innovation jungle is to make them understand. Now, thump your Tarzan chest because you just learned something really important.

---

[4] That's right—one of the most important innovation axioms delivered by Meat Loaf. You are welcome.

Disruptor rule: Insight first. Idea second.

*If you are stubbornly convinced that people **love** your product or service, you will never find an insight big enough to get the market's attention.*

CUSTOMER EXPERIENCE: A LOVE-HATE STORY

It isn't just products and services that Disruptors love to hate. They are also now addressing the many ridiculously bad experiences we have learned to ignore or put up with as consumers. They are turning awfulness into opportunities to grow their profits, brands and customer loyalty while leaving their competitors behind.

See if any of this sounds amusing and/or sadly familiar:

Your typical day starts with an artfully pierced and tattooed 20-something rolling his eyes while correcting you for ordering your $4+ cup of coffee the wrong way.

Later, you may hear "the doctor is ready to see you now," when he really should be apologizing for making you sit in the aptly named waiting room (surrounded by a cesspool of germs) for 45 minutes—AGAIN.

Next, move on to the brick and mortar superstore where you'll have to say "no" at least three times to the commission-driven offer of a protection plan, a credit card application and the club card.

You have a business trip? Lucky you. TSA stands for "thousands standing around," so it will only take 35 minutes for the employees to watch the one person who is actually working make you get undressed and rifle through your carry-on.

The taxi driver will claim that his credit card machine is broken because he prefers cash (you took a cab because the airport insisted you walk an extra mile to get a rideshare).

At the hotel, you'll be charged for internet connection in your room, even though the people in the lobby are getting it for free. You hang your towel (because they asked you to save the planet), but they take it, wash it and replace it with a clean one anyway.

Thirsty? Instead of touting the purity of the room's tap water, you'll have an option of a $6 or $12 bottle of water that you will pass on because there is now a glob of plastic trash floating in the Pacific Ocean bigger than France.

Want coffee? Great! First unwrap 14 items to create a 12-ounce cup.

On the flight home, the overhead is full, so you must check your bag. You will be seated next to a 400-pound man, eating a foot-long, garlic-infused Meat Monster. He is poured into the (cheaper) middle seat and will drop into a "carb coma" during the climb and drool on you for the remainder of the flight. At this point, you need a cocktail, but unlike your cab driver, they no longer take cash on board.

For years, the providers of these products and services have turned a deaf ear to our complaints. Due to a lack of options, information and control, people like you and me just put up with one bad customer experience after another.

Enter the Disruptors who are, thankfully, bringing those days to an end.

That rumble you hear in the distance is a tectonic shift of epic proportions, fueled by fed-up consumers who now have the technology, information, social networks and choices to create the experiences they want.

WHY CHANGING THE CUSTOMER EXPERIENCE (CX) IS SO HARD

If you're looking for higher margins, more brand loyalty and a starting point to introduce innovation within your organization, creating a wonderful customer experience is the place to begin because it quickly gives you an unfair competitive advantage.

But as you know, it is often difficult to change the course of a business that has been doing things the same way, for the same people, with (up until recently) comfortable margins for many years.

Why is it so difficult to change? Here are four unfortunately common reasons:

Leadership is not aligned. Leadership in your organization needs to be crystal clear on the experience your consumers want and what you are going to offer. That means spending in-depth time with your customers—and the people you would like to be your customers—to understand their needs. You can't stop with answers like: "I want a faster transaction." You need to know what customers mean by "faster" and how they expect "faster" to feel.

Your interpretation of the need is wrong. Too often, people miss the nuances in translating perceived needs into the correct best experiences. For example, hotels may rush to give away free internet connections when it wasn't the cost but the complexity of getting online that had customers frustrated. They might be willing to pay for it if all it took was one click of a mouse.

You don't involve the organization. People support what they create. By opening up customer experience initiatives to a larger group of people in your organization, you make the ideas stronger and overcome the inertia and cultural antibodies companies have to change.

You don't test in market. The desire to have a "fully baked" solution before you roll it out robs you of the consumer feedback loop that would make the idea better and more appealing to your customers.

That's all the bad news.

The good news is that these challenges can be overcome. For proof, you don't have to look any further than a health insurance company, of all places.

The global research firm Forrester awarded Blue Cross Blue Shield of Michigan (BCBSM) with their Outside-In Award, which is given to organizations "that excel at the practices needed for planning, creating, and managing a great customer experience." This award was given to BCBSM on the heels of a two-year journey that started by asking their customer's customer what was missing in their health care experience and then (and only then) responding with relevant new products and services.

I am proud that Blue Cross Blue Shield of Michigan is our client. But the bigger point is: Winning an award for customer understanding in health care is notable because it is, thankfully, a sign of things to come.

CUSTOMER EXPERIENCE: THE PROCESS

The smartest companies are now working hard to manage their customers' experiences with their products and services in order to delight and retain them.

So how do you do it?

A successful customer experience cycle looks like this:

Let's take all parts of the circle one at a time.

Connect and Attract

This is your chance to establish a real connection with your customers. Your mother was right: You never get a second chance to make a first impression to demonstrate your relevance to the consumers. Extra credit if you meet them where they hate you the most.

Orient

This is your opportunity to be crystal clear on the possible ways you can serve your customers better—to make the hate go away—by requiring the least amount of effort for them to change or adapt to you. Most companies trip over this part because employees are so knowledgeable about their product or service that they can't empathize with consumers who are new to it. That's expertise and confirmation bias at its worst. Here you want to invite, allow and anticipate exploration, curiosity and questions on the customer's terms.

Transact

You deliver a valuable activity in exchange for time, money, information, etc. The best exchanges are uniquely and delightfully positive, setting the bar for future encounters.

Extend and Retain

Your customers come back for more, and you again exceed their expectations in ways that do not have to only be associated with the product or service itself. For example, think of the last time you discovered a great vacation location or reliable service provider using Travelocity or HomeAdvisor. How often did you follow this discovery with a referral that sounded something like this? "You should call Pete's Plumbing. I found him on HomeAdvisor.com." This is where the love affair becomes real. You now are working on a meaningful relationship with your customers.

Advocate

Your customers actively communicate their love for you with others. Give your customers permission and a suggestion for where to talk about you.

SHARE THE JOURNEY

Ideas are just like our kids. They deserve good parenting, too.

Too many companies rely only on their sales staff—or worse, completely on channel partners—to tell them what their customers' experiences are like. This is like asking a pilot how a flight went. From his perspective, the plane landed safely, so things went great. He has no idea that the flight attendants ran out of drinks somewhere over Tulsa or that the guy in front of you rammed his chair back, spilling coffee on your lap and laptop. And he is clueless about the fact that the overhead bins were full after "boarding group 2" entered the plane, leaving 63 people standing in the Jetway after the plane landed, waiting for their carry-ons and worrying if they will make their connections. The point: Empathy is critical, and it comes from you sharing every part of the journey with your customer. Too often we think innovation needs to be something that has fancy buttons that you plug in. The best Disruptors see possibilities to improve every touch point—from point of sale to product to helpline to billing experience.

FOCUS

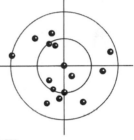

You can't be all things to all people. If your FAQ (frequently asked questions) list has dozens and dozens of questions, it is a pretty good indication that you need to focus more on what you can uniquely and magically deliver to your customers. Customer intimacy means you have learned what matters most to your customers and therefore can guide the conversation and create the best experience.

Great brands have used customer experiences to create a "love affair" with their customers. Creating a love affair with your customers takes time, patience and empathy. Remember, this is a journey that involves new discoveries, exploration and mutual benefit. There will be ups and downs that you, your team and your customers will experience along the way, and you need to pull each other along to create relationships grounded in trust and loyalty.

Customer experience experts understand that a "love affair" with your consumers is the ultimate brand advantage because, in life and business, love conquers all.

DISRUPTOR TAKEAWAYS AND HACKS

1. **Disruptors embrace the hate.** Disruptors move quickly from complaining to action to ideas. They see things that they hate as an opportunity to make (sometimes dramatic) changes for the better. Typical companies spend most of their time listening to their most loyal and delighted customers. They work to make those customers love them even more. But Disruptors go looking for haters because they intuitively sense great opportunity.

2. **Love is blind. Hate is scalable.** The people who love you tell you what you want to hear. The people who hate what you are offering tell you what you NEED to hear, at least if you want to avoid being blindsided by a competitor. And the greater the hate is, the more meaningful the opportunity. Turn a large group of haters into lovers, and you are a Disruptor.

3. **Confirmation bias kills.** When we are experts in an industry, we unconsciously look for evidence that we are right. Look for new entries into your industry or business for a fresh perspective about what's really happening.

DISRUPTOR TAKEAWAYS AND HACKS (cont.)

4. **Think macro, not myopic.** What business are you really in? What business should you be in? To get the answers to these questions, move from a myopic view of your purpose to a far broader one.

5. **B2B is dead.** Successful companies run the risk of focusing too much on their current products and distributors, losing sight of the constant and dramatically changing needs of their customer base.

6. **Parallel engineer.** The sad irony of being an expert is that it keeps you from seeing possibility even when it is right in front of you. After all, you know what works, what doesn't, what you can afford, what's been tried in the past. So instead of relying only on your own expertise, find other experts who are solving similar challenges to yours but in different fields. Then go ask them what they may be missing.

7. **Insight first. Idea second.** Invention is starting with an idea and then looking for someone who wants it. Innovation is starting with a meaningful insight (the more hate the better) and then finding a novel way to solve it. Be an innovator.

(Please take notes here to make the author believe
he is actually delivering some value.)

(Thank you.)

EMBRACE THE HATE TO INNOVATE

Chapter 8

Choose Abundance. Screw Scarcity.

"Eureka!"

In April 2005, Barrett Ersek had his first breakthrough moment, and I was incredibly lucky to be there to see it.[1]

Let me set the scene.

I was sitting in a classroom with my friends at a Massachusetts Institute of Technology (MIT) facility in suburban Boston. We were attending the entrepreneurial conclave Birthing of Giants (BOG), and we were captivated, as always, by thought leader Verne Harnish who was leading the class. As I write this, our class has been meeting in the same room, every year, for a week at a time, since 2002. BOG (an organization started at MIT in 1996), in partnership with *Inc.* magazine and the Young Entrepreneurs' Organization (called EO today), is an educational program for owners of growing companies.

Before attending this BOG meeting, I thought business success came from a combination of intelligence, connections, hard work, cash and picking the right market trends.

Barrett taught me that Disruptors had another tool in their toolbox. Disruptors have the ability to manufacture serendipity, and Barrett did it with the best of them.

Even in a room full of entrepreneurs (i.e., the "crazy ones"), Barrett stood out as one of the craziest. Much to his parents'

---

[1] As you will see, "blessed" might actually be a better word.

disappointment, he had dropped out of college to continue running his lawn care business, Happy Lawn, that he started in high school. Barrett, a class clown, just couldn't bring himself to sit in college lectures and learn about business when he already had one that needed his love. So he left school and used grit and determination to turn his small company into a multimillion-dollar company.

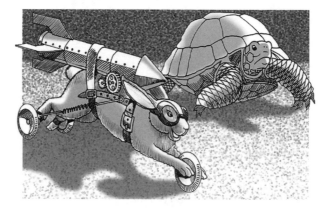

However, years later, he felt stuck and like an imposter in the class. Although he was making decent money, Happy Lawn wasn't growing like some of his classmates' businesses were, and he didn't know what to do about it.

It turns out the idea of applying chemicals and fertilizers to lawns requires a clunky, complicated business model. To make it work, his staff spent time calling homes, scheduling appointments, measuring lawns, providing quotes, closing a small percentage of the quotes, and then sending out teams to do the work. And then you waited four to eight weeks to get paid.

It was an expensive, inefficient business. Barrett spent $275 to acquire one client worth $400 in revenue. Gross margin was about 50 percent. Do the math and you see it would take six quarters to just pay for the customer acquisition costs. Oh, and he had a 20 percent attrition rate. Ouch.

Maybe he should have stayed in college.

But during this BOG meeting, Barrett was struck by inspiration—his first "panacea moment." He abruptly stood up in the middle of a lecture, apologized to Verne, and said to the rest of us,

"Sorry guys, I've got to go." I remember thinking something must have happened to one of his kids and being concerned.

A call to Barrett a couple days later confirmed that everything was fine; he had just thought of an idea that could not wait and wanted to begin working on it immediately. (We all understood. That's typically how entrepreneurs roll. They don't wait; they just start to build and experiment.)

For the next 12 months, Barrett researched, built, tested and eventually launched a business model that would disrupt the entire lawn care industry. The following year, Barrett came back to MIT, not as the jokester college dropout, but as a guy who had realized that he really could change the world; he was watching it happen.

Like many other Disruptors, Barrett had manufactured serendipity.

I'll tell you what he did in a moment, but I want to make this point first: You must be open to the possibility of providence.

The year before, Verne Harnish had been talking about X factors. An X factor is some new technology, process or shortcut that, when implemented, creates 10 times or more unfair competitive advantage against your competition.

Barrett was open to any idea that could help him. He had been racking his brain, trying to figure out how to transform lawn care. He was thinking about his pinch points. He was trying to reimagine his business. And he was looking for anything—literally anything—to give his lawn care company an unfair competitive advantage.

The idea that caused Barrett to bolt out of the room was simple but bold. His creation was a software solution that combined satellite imagery with an estimation tool.

Instead of calling to schedule an appointment, sending someone to measure a lawn to provide a quote, working to close a deal, doing the work and then billing a job, he could combine multiple steps.

Now, his best people would simply call a customer, quote a job using real-time satellite imagery of their lawn and the software he created, take a credit card number and close the deal. And since they were trained salespeople, not lawn care guys, they were better at closing deals, extending contracts and getting paid in real time.

The numbers don't lie. Barrett's innovation moved his inbound close rate from 20 percent to 80 percent. It moved his average closing time from three weeks to three days. It dropped his cost per sale from $275 to $50.

Within a year, Barrett had quadrupled his billings. Eventually, his solution and his company were purchased by Scott's, making Barrett—a college dropout—a multimillionaire.

Let's stop to think about this for a moment. What gave Barrett Ersek—a lawn care guy, college dropout, class clown, average kid from Philadelphia—the right to change the world? Or, put differently, why would Barrett even think he had a chance to change the world?

The answer is pretty simple. Barrett was not only open to serendipity, but he also had an abundant mindset.

Barrett taught me that success came from more than just intelligence, connections, hard work, cash and picking the right market trends. It came from believing you could change the world. It came from an abundant mindset.

THE ABUNDANT MINDSET

"Everything happens for a reason."

"One door closes, another one opens."

"Don't worry, I'll make more...."

"I am grateful for this challenge because _____."

> If you think you will succeed or think you will fail, you are correct.
> – Henry Ford

All of these sayings might sound like just the platitudes of a starry-eyed optimist, but here in Entrepreneurland, they are indicators that someone has the abundant mindset.

In order to be an entrepreneur, inventor or innovator, you must view life through the lens of abundance. You must see opportunity where others see obstacles and stop signs. Having an abundant mindset means that you are so pulled by possibility that risk speeds you up instead of slows you down. Simply put, for an entrepreneur, abundance is what enables you to change the world.

And this mindset is one of the most generative superhero powers of the Disruptor.

Maybe the easiest way to understand the abundant mindset is to look at the exact opposite way of thinking: the scarcity mindset.

 That mindset makes you believe that things are permanent and unchangeable. Your imagined scarcity of opportunity fuels envy and negative thinking. You are not generous with your time or money because you are convinced you are going to run out of clock and cash.

You'll hear people with the scarcity mindset say things like:

"I'm not smart enough."

"The odds are against me."

"I can't afford it."

"Those guys are sure lucky."

"Maybe someday…."

Financial services thought leader Garrett Gunderson taught me about the scarcity mindset by talking about personal investments, like our 401(k) plans, where scarcity is unknowingly programmed into us.

Financial advisors around the world preach "save, save, save, lest you run out of money someday. What if you live to 80? 90? 100…120? You sure don't want to be a burden on those you love."

So people with the scarcity mindset put off that vacation, that invention, that business they want to start, that dream…and "save their money for a rainy day"—a saying that actually dates back to the 1600s, so you can see the scarcity mindset has been around for a long time.

But wouldn't it be better to climb Machu Piccu, view the Sistine Chapel or travel to see your favorite band while you can still walk, see and hear? Scarcity thinking keeps all this from happening.

Fortunately, not everyone has the scarcity mindset. So while some are putting off climbing the mountain, seeing the Vatican or enjoying the band, professional investors with an abundant mindset are taking their investment dollars and creating generative ways to invest in vehicles that cash flow that money.

Here are two options to illustrate the point:

1. You could invest your entire savings into a 401(k) and hope for 5 to 8 percent annual return. If you obtain it, your advisor will beg you to wait as long as possible before you touch the cash that is accumulating. After all, you would not want to run out of money. So you'll likely be more than 70 years old before you allow yourself to enjoy any of your hard-earned savings.

Or:

2. You could take the same money, invest in rental properties that spit off 5 to 8 percent a year in cash, while the properties themselves appreciate in value. So by the time you are 70 years old, you've never gone a month without cash and, oh yeah, you now have properties worth more than what you paid for them.

The person with the scarcity mindset will likely embrace scenario No. 1, while someone with the abundant mindset would go for No. 2.

IDEAS
WELCOME
FROM
ANYWHERE

GRATEFULNESS: THE KEY TO AN ABUNDANT MINDSET

After selling his lawn care company, Barrett Ersek met Brother David, who explained to Barrett why he was naturally inclined to an abundant mindset: Barrett was an abundantly grateful person.

Barrett now believes gratefulness starts early. "My parents were really good at pointing out little things that I should appreciate," he says. "So as I got older, even if I was sweating and swatting mosquitoes doing lawn work, I usually found something to be happy about, like the sunset or how much better the beer would taste at the end of the day. Come to think of it, maybe it was my subconscious that came up with my first company name: Happy Lawn."

In Brother David, Barrett found a kindred spirit who had thought more deeply about gratefulness than he had. More important, Brother David had mastered how to maintain it during difficult circumstances. This would prove to be very valuable to Barrett a few years later, as we will see.

Brother David was born in Vienna, Austria, as Franz Kuno Steindl-Rast. Although he spent his early years in a small village in the Alps, the timing of his teenage years meant being drafted into the occupying Nazi army. To survive the emotional burden of being enlisted to fight a war he did not believe in, against those he considered to be his brothers and sisters (he was of partial Jewish descent), Franz decided to be grateful for something every day—a song from a bird; dew drops from a plant; a hug from a friend.... For Franz, gratefulness literally became a practice of survival.

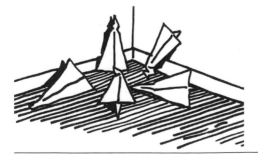

Fortunately, he managed to slip away from his military company and ended up being hidden by his mother until the occupation ended. Franz never fought on the front lines.

After the war, Franz's curiosity moved him to study art, anthropology and psychology. In Europe, he received both an MA from the Vienna Academy of Fine Arts and a Ph.D. from the University of Vienna.

Some of Franz's family had moved to the United States and he followed them to New York State. It was in Elmira, New York, at Mount Savior Monastery, a Benedictine community, where he became "Brother David."

He was not done learning. Brother David became a Postdoctoral Fellow at Cornell University. After 12 years of monastic training and studies in philosophy and theology, in 1967, Brother David was sent by his abbot to participate in a Buddhist-Christian program approved by the Vatican. After studying under legendary Zen teachers, he co-founded the Center for Spiritual Studies in 1968 and received the 1975 Martin Buber Award for his achievements in building bridges between religious traditions.

Brother David is now on a mission to spread a message of love and gratefulness. He wants to make gratitude a core value of corporations. He has spoken around the globe to a full spectrum of humanity. His audiences range from starving students in Zaire to faculty at Harvard and Columbia Universities; from Buddhist monks and Papago Indians to German intellectuals and Navy Cadets at Annapolis; from missionaries on Polynesian islands to gatherings at the United Nations.

When they met, Barrett Ersek had plenty of questions for Brother David.

For one, Barrett wondered how an aggressive, scrappy entrepreneur from Philly could get into heaven. Not surprisingly, Brother David had thought deeply about the topic.

"Barrett, heaven is available to the Muslim and to the Jew. Heaven is even available to the Catholic (Brother David laughed since this was his path). Heaven is even available to the atheist, but often the atheist doesn't find heaven because he is full of conflict, full of pushing away. Religions are belief systems designed to help people find their way.

"To whom much is given, much is required."

But faith...faith is trust in life...trust that everything life brings you is a gift, even when it seems like a pile of sh** (laughing again). If you can truly embrace adversity in your life as a gift, if you can trust that life is bringing you a gift, even when it is not obvious how, then you remove your heart and your soul from anxiety and stress and conflict, and you replace it with creativity and peace. If you can trust that everything life brings you is a gift, you can have heaven on earth."

Brother David went on to say, "If you can trust that everything life brings you is a gift, then you will trust that even death is a gift, because after all, what does life bring everyone eventually but death? And if you can trust that even death is a gift, then surely you will go to heaven."

Barrett did not consider himself a religious man at the time of this conversation. So he was stunned when, at that moment, he began to weep uncontrollably. Brother David knowingly reached out, gave Barrett a hug and said, "I see you understand."

Barrett has never looked at adversity the same again. Brother David had helped him understand the power of gratefulness and its role in abundant thinking.

THIS THINKING PAYS OFF

Ten years later, Barrett needed to lean heavily on his abundant mindset.

Back in the lawn care business, he found himself in a situation where fertilizer costs, his biggest expense, were sky-rocketing. Barrett, in an attempt to control costs, bought in bulk and stockpiled his warehouse with 10 times the amount of fertilizer that he would ordinarily carry.

Unfortunately, the warehouse storing the fertilizer burnt to the ground. No one was hurt, but Ersek didn't have nearly enough insurance to cover the cost of the fertilizer he had lost. Furthermore, it looked like he would be forced to purchase replacement fertilizer at much higher costs.

"Instead of losing hope, I decided to be grateful for the adversity and to think of it as a gift," he recalls, drawing on the wisdom of Brother David.

Barrett's positive attitude paid off. The burning down of his warehouse forced him to seek solutions he wouldn't otherwise have tried. As part of his quest, he stumbled across an organic fertilizer called Holganix, which had been created by Stephan T. Lange.

Barrett discovered that the product allowed him to dramatically reduce the amount of nitrates, phosphates and pesticides he used in treating lawns, eliminating what was seen as a necessary evil in his industry. He quickly became Lange's largest customer and, over time, Barrett became more and more involved with Lange's business.

"I couldn't understand why Lange's product wasn't mainstream!" he recalls.

"What I needed to do was create a community of Holganix users committed to changing the green grass industry," Barrett says in describing "panacea moment" No. 2. He joined forces with Lange, and Holganix (the company) was born.

Holganix opened its doors in 2010 with a goal of eliminating negative externalities to the tune of 100 million pounds of nitrates, 25 million pounds of phosphates and 100 million pounds of concentrated pesticides from entering the universe by Earth Day 2020. "At the time, that goal seemed impossible," Barrett recalls. "Today, the company has notable users including the Pittsburgh Pirates, the Tennessee Titans, the Boston Red Sox, along with world championship golf courses, national lawn care companies and Ivy League universities. It's no longer about whether or how we are going to reach our goal of breaking our industry's environmental bottleneck, but how soon!"

PRACTICE GRATEFULNESS

In 1872, Charles Darwin first posed the idea that emotional responses influence our feelings. He wrote: "The free expression by outward signs of an emotion intensifies it."

The esteemed 19th-century psychologist William James went so far as to assert that if a person does not express an emotion, he has not felt it at all. Although few scientists would agree with such a statement today, there is evidence that emotions involve more than just the brain. The face, in particular, appears to play a big role.

In February 2018, psychologists at the University of Cardiff in Wales found that people whose ability to frown is compromised by cosmetic Botox injections are happier, on average, than people who can frown.

The researchers administered an anxiety and depression questionnaire to women, half of whom had received frown-inhibiting Botox injections. The Botox recipients reported feeling happier and less anxious in general. More important, they did not report feeling any more attractive, which suggests that  the emotional effects were not driven by a psychological boost that could come from the treatment's cosmetic nature.

"It would appear that the way we feel emotions isn't just restricted to our brain—there are parts of our bodies that help and reinforce the feelings we're having," says Professor Michael Lewis, a co-author of the study. "It's like a feedback loop." In a related study from March 2018, scientists at the Technical University of Munich in Germany scanned Botox recipients with fMRI machines while asking them to mimic angry faces. They found that the Botox subjects had much lower activity in the brain circuits involved in emotional processing and responses—in the amygdala, hypothalamus and parts of the brain stem—as compared with controls who had not received treatment.

The concept works the opposite way too—enhancing emotions rather than suppressing them. People who frown during an unpleasant procedure report feeling more pain than those who do not, according to a study published in May 2008 in the *Journal of Pain*. Researchers applied heat to the forearms of 29 participants who were asked to either make unhappy, neutral or relaxed faces during the procedure. Those who exhibited negative expressions reported being in more pain than the other two groups.

Lewis, who was not involved in that research, says he plans to study the effect that Botox injections have on pain perception. "It's possible," he says, "that people may feel less pain if they're unable to express it."

No one yet knows why our facial expressions influence our emotions as they seem to. The associations in our mind between how we feel and how we react may be so strong that our expressions simply end up reinforcing our emotions. There may be no evolutionary reason for the connection. Even so, our faces do seem to communicate our states of mind not only to others but also to ourselves. "I smile, so I must be happy."

The research and Barrett's experience, with gratitude, have convinced me that your mindset is one of the key reasons—if not THE sole reason—that will determine your success.

As Henry Ford once said, "Whether you think you can, or you think you can't—you're right."

DISRUPTOR TAKEAWAYS AND HACKS

1. **There is a saying, alternately attributed to Buddha.** Siddhartha Gautama Shakyamuni and the theosophists that goes: "When the student is ready, the teacher will appear." You need to make yourself open to serendipity.[2]

2. **Everything is an opportunity...** absolutely everything.

3. **Let me remind you of one of my favorite Steve Jobs quotes:**

> "Those who are crazy enough to think they can change the world usually do."
>
> Steve Jobs

---

[2] That's right. I just quoted Buddha. My fifth grade teacher, Sister Helen, may be rolling her eyes in heaven.

DISRUPTOR TAKEAWAYS AND HACKS (cont.)

4. Avoid the achievement gap. Serial entrepreneur David Rich does a weekly exercise with an accountability partner. Starting Sunday, he will send an email with three to five achievements he wants to make happen in the next week. At the end of the week, he and his partner discuss what they accomplished and how to make further progress through specific actions.

David says that Dan Sullivan of the Strategic Coach made him aware that exercises that help leaders notice their progress keep them from falling into "the achievement gap." In other words, by constantly marking your progress, your attitude and outlook stay positive and abundant.

DISRUPTOR TAKEAWAYS AND HACKS (cont.)

5. Start your day abundantly. Best-selling author and leadership guru Kevin Kruse starts every day with a smile because of one simple thing he does. Before he tackles his "to-do" list, or anything else, he thinks of three things that he is grateful for—which usually includes having all of his senses, healthy kids and a full tummy. Says Kevin, "I can risk everything in my pursuit of entrepreneurship because if I lose it all, I know I'll still have everything I need to be happy."

Kevin's gratitude practice made me smile. So I mentioned it to my wife, Ruthie, who quickly responded, "Yes! Give thanks in all circumstances. That's biblical." Turns out she is correct. I looked it up. Thessalonians 5:18.

(Study after study shows that if you give your brain
a break, it will surprise you with a big idea.)

Chapter 9

Purpose First (Profit Second)

Did someone scream gun?

Christina Harbridge was sure she heard someone yelling in the lobby. Concerned but curious, she ignored the butterflies in her stomach and walked toward the front door of the collection agency where she worked.

As she headed toward the lobby, everyone else was running the other way. Just as Christina turned the corner to enter the waiting area by the front door, someone yelled, "Look out. He's got a gun."

She froze. But it was too late. The man with a gun saw her.

HOW WE GOT HERE

Life wasn't supposed to be so complicated. Christina was 19 years old and in college studying chemistry. Her plan going in was to be a typical college kid: study hard, party hard, make some new friends and maybe even meet a nice boy or two.

But her dad's illness had quickly changed everything. Her hero was rapidly slipping away with Parkinson's disease, and he needed expensive care. Driven by her dad's condition, Christina had scoured the want ads, desperately looking for a job that would pay enough to help get him into the nicest facility possible.

When she first saw the word "collections" in the paper, she thought it meant "antiques" and was excited because she liked collecting old things. Better still, the job paid twice the minimum wage! She quickly found out that the ad was for a debt collection agency and she would be filing a lot of paperwork. Worse, she would also be working in company full of people who were really nice in the lunchroom but mean on the phone.

The company gave bonuses based on money collected and believed the meaner they were on the phone, the more they collected, which meant the more they got paid.

So the employees at the collection agency were being mean "on purpose." The company's unwritten mission, its purpose, was to relentlessly badger people who refused to pay their bills until they coughed up the dough because they couldn't take it anymore.

Apparently, the man shouting in the lobby couldn't take it any-more—and had decided to end the relationship with the collection agency creatively.

Christina tried to ignore the thought of bullet wounds, as the angry man with the gun screamed that everyone was about to "F**ing die."

Christina didn't like F***ing guns, and she didn't want to F***ing die.

She tasted the fear coming up from her stomach. But remarkably, Christina pushed back her instinct to flee and slowly approached the shooter. Her dad was a political activist and had always taught her to walk toward aggression. (He meant dogs, but whatever.) Softly, Christina asked the man with the gun why he was so upset. He yelled back something about the company ruining his life.

He had come looking for the person who kept calling his home. He was going to kill somebody and then maybe even kill himself.

Christina nodded as she looked into the man's eyes. Then some-thing strange happened. Her eyes began watering. She was upset too.

Christina said, "Look, right now all you owe is money. Are we worth a felony to you? Let's figure this out."

Christina's questions were challenging, loving and sincere. She really felt the man's pain. She could see how much he loved his family. Worse, she believed her employer had driven him over the edge. She felt partly responsible. And she believed it was now her duty to find a way to shift his thinking and help him recover the life he wanted.

The questions tilted the gunman's perspective.

He exhaled and answered, "No, you people are not worth throwing my life away." He reached into his other pocket.

Christina held her breath. She figured he was finished with her and was going for his weapon. Instead, he pulled out a checkbook. He wrote a check, apologized and walked away.

So did Christina.

The event in the lobby moved her to closely examine the collection industry at large. In the course of her study in school (Christina switched and became an economics major), she wondered what would happen if the collection industry focused on helping people rather than callously driving them into submission. What if all those mean calls were NICE and spread goodwill? What if she trained collection people to be empathetic instead of intimidating? What if she took an irrational idea and made a business out of it?

Her activist father believed that the best way to change a system was to "infiltrate it"—in other words, by becoming part of it. So when Christina told him about her irrational idea to start a "nice" collection agency, he smiled and responded, "People will hate you for it; you have to do it!"

So driven by her own "what ifs" and her father's encouragement, Christina—a natural Disruptor—opened a collection agency in California in 1994. It became the best "infiltration scheme" ever.

From the beginning, Christina vowed to put purpose first and profits second. Her vision was simple: To be the nicest collection agency in the world. (Actually, it was to be the nicest COMPANY in the world.) In her words, "The human relationship is the true currency." Christina figured that

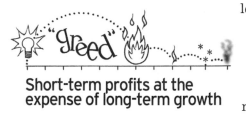

Short-term profits at the expense of long-term growth

her new company could be nice and still make a reasonable profit. Maybe she wouldn't get rich, but she'd get by, make some money and feel good about doing it. She wanted to be a conscious capitalist, the term used for those who choose to follow a business strategy where they seek to benefit society in addition to making money.

(We will talk a little bit more about this later in the chapter.) She was willing to surrender a couple of percentage points of profit in order to spread happiness and hopefully see a few less gun-wielding men in her lobby. She figured that "nice" may not collect as much money, but it was the right thing to do, AND some companies would want the last contact they had with their customers to be positive.

PURPOSE TESTED

Her dad was right; people did hate the idea.[1] When Christina's company helped a client who was in over her head file for bankruptcy, an opportunist attorney filed a class action lawsuit claiming that Christina's company was using kindness as a deceptive business practice to manipulate unsuspecting people. No joke.

The lawsuit could not have come at a worse time. It was early days and cash flow was terrible. Christina had a maxed-out line of credit, huge credit card debt, no money in the bank and no Plan B (yeah, pun intended). She was running on fumes, barely making payroll and scared as hell.

But she had a purpose, and it gave her the courage to press on. Her lawyer arranged a deposition in which Christina was asked to explain why she had started her company and why she measured success by thank-you cards from the people who owed money instead of money collected. When Christina was finished, her attorney turned to the opposing counsel and said, "You can see her passion. Everyone can. So will the judge and the jury. I DARE you to put her on the stand. You are going to lose, and you are going to lose very, very badly."

Christina's lawyer was right. They won the case. And ensuing PR coverage turned the lawsuit into a sales gift from the heavens. The company was suddenly extremely profitable and extremely popular.

---

[1] If at least some people are not reacting negatively to your idea, you do not have a disruptive idea.

Remarkably, her purpose first plan worked much better than she expected.

By 2001, her company was named one of the Bay Area's Top 150 Fastest-Growing Privately Held Companies.

In 2002, they were a finalist for Excellence in Business Award, and then again in 2003, although Salesforce edged them out for the win.

By 2003, Christina was named as the honorary co-chair of the Business Advisory Council in Washington, D.C. She received the National Leadership Award, and her company was one of the three finalists for the San Francisco Chamber of Commerce's Emerging Growth Award.

By 2005, Christina was selected as one of Collectionindusty.com's "Young Guns." Oh, the irony.

At the heart of Christina's business idea was her insight that the purpose of a collection call was NOT to collect money. It was to establish enough of a relationship to hear the truth. So she coached her people to turn confrontation into helpful conversation—to help people who creditors claimed owed money understand if there really was a debt to be paid; help them dispute their bill if it was in doubt; and help them figure out ways to pay it if it was not.

Christina understood that being helpful first was a brand promise the large companies that hired her would find attractive. After all, if your company can take the ugliest part of its business—collections—and make people feel good about it, who wouldn't want to work with you?

In the end, Christina wound up building one of the fastest-growing and most profitable collection companies.

Christina measured everything. And since she knew that 71 percent of incoming calls were people who were yelling, she spent four times as much as her competitors training her people to manage anxiety, stress and conflict. One result of this training was that their average calls took 5.2 minutes instead of the industry's 2 minutes. Most of her competitors saw that as an unnecessary expense. Christina—rightly—saw it as an asset. Her firm collected 32.2 percent of the money owed instead of the industry average 9.9 percent.

In the end, Christina's employees got thank-you cards from debtors. They got invited to their weddings. Debtors would bring their kids in to meet their bill collector. Her people enjoyed their jobs.

PROOF THIS WORKS

Here are just a few examples of how Christina's team at her company stayed on purpose:

1. At the beginning of each day, for 30 minutes, the employees each shared stories of when they had "caught" each other doing something positive or extraordinary. This 30 minutes was a way to remind them that people were kind and prepare them for the seven out of 10 calls that would involve people screaming at them.

2. Employees received bonuses for thank-you cards received (they were not allowed to ask for them) rather than money collected. Christina noted that the person with the most cards received always had the most money collected—fancy that!

3. The company put a toy box up in the lobby for kids who came in with their parents who owed money. The reasoning? The kids deserved a gift for being part of the process of resolving their family's debt.

4. A secret debtor fund was created. Employees nominated debtors each month who were in an exceptionally rough spot and trying really hard. They asked the debtor to sign an agreement not to say anything—"this is about you; we don't want any

publicity"—and then the company would pay off his or her debts. They never let anyone know they did this. For the collectors, making these calls was a highlight of their jobs.

Note: To most collection companies, this idea was like committing financial suicide. The bill collector pays off your bills for you? What kind of idea was that? To Christina's company, it was about doing business "on purpose."

As you can imagine, all of these activities created a culture that was extraordinary. They worked in large part because Christina led by example. One day, Christina saw a "Your Mother Doesn't Work Here—Do Your Dishes!" sign in the kitchen. She called an impromptu company meeting and announced, "You all have terribly stressful jobs. So from this moment forward, I am going to do all the dishes. This is my gift for you. I am not being passive aggressive, I want to give you this gift."

The next day as she entered the kitchen, Christina found a pair of fur-lined dish gloves and a glammed-out apron waiting for her. There was a boom box on the counter with a collection of her favorite music, and there was a thank-you letter from her team.

But there were no dishes in the sink.

And there were never dishes in the sink again. As much as Christina wanted to do the dishes, she never got the chance. Her offer of service had reignited in everyone else the desire to serve.

Acts of service went well beyond the kitchen. Months later when an employee needed a kidney, three co-workers went and got tested to see if they were matches for a donation.

You get the idea. The purpose of the company had infected the culture. It naturally had attracted the types of people who wanted to be nice. And it created a platform for extraordinary and disruptively nice services.

"Wherever you stand, be the soul of that place."
Rumi, a 13th-century poet and jurist

In 2006, Christina sold her thriving company so she could spend more time with her infant son.

Today, Christina is a recognized thought leader. Still, on purpose, she writes about, speaks about and teaches people how to invest in and grow their most important relationships.

WHY DISRUPTORS START WITH "WHY"

In 2010, I was running the global brand boot camp for the Young Presidents' Organization (YPO). As a favor, I asked my friend Simon Sinek to join our gathering in Chicago and present on his now-famous concept and first book "Start With Why." At the time, the idea of purpose-driven companies was still relatively novel, but I'd noticed some of my most successful business friends leading with purpose. So I thought it was important that this group of leaders explored the idea together.

Simon had arrived early that day and watched quietly from the corner as the 50 or so presidents from a myriad of industries formally introduced themselves. During the introductions, the door swung open. In walked an older gentleman talking loudly into a pink, bedazzled flip phone. He had white spiked hair, leather pants, ornate cowboy boots and a studded, red leather jacket. Since the session was at the Four Seasons, I actually thought he might be a rock star who had stumbled into the wrong room. As Simon and the rest of us looked on in stunned silence, he loudly clanged through the breakfast buffet while he talked on the phone. All the while, he was completely oblivious to the 50-plus executives staring at him. He eventually took a seat in the back of the room with his breakfast plate, unaware of the disruption he had created.

Simon seemed amused and winked at me from the corner. I was not amused because I was supposed to be running a tight ship, and I had no idea who the person was.

At this point, I remembered that I was supposed to be leading, so I cleared my throat and asked the people in the front of the room to continue to introduce themselves.

The morning moved on and Simon watched another purpose-driven leader named Burt Jacobs talk about his company named Life is Good. Burt had taken the idea of selling (out of a van) T-shirts promoting gratefulness and optimism and turned it into a $140 million company that was more concerned with helping sick kids than selling shirts. Incredible.[2]

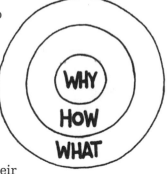

Eventually, it was time for Simon to present, and he did not disappoint.

Simon drew his Golden Circle™ framework on a flip pad to help explain how good leaders start with "what"; they are very clear about a product or service they think you should buy. Better leaders start with "how"; they have a process or system for delivering their product or service that makes them superior to their competition. But the greatest leaders of all start with "why"; they have created a purpose so powerful that it attracts the right people/customers — the ones who share their mission or values — to their product or service.

The presidents in the room were engaged but confused. I could see they were trying to wrap their heads around the idea of leading through purpose instead of profits. They started challenging Simon's thesis. Dr. Tom Shuler of Virginia Spine Institute commented: "Our purpose is to provide the greatest patient…blah…blah…interdisciplinary

---

[2] Life IS Good!

...blah...blah...". (Tom later told me that people's eyes would glaze over when he described what he did. Mine did. But luckily, Simon's didn't.)

Simon paused dramatically and said, "No, that's not a purpose. That's a 'what'; that's what you do. People don't buy what you do; they buy why you do it. It sounds like you are in the making lives better business."[3] He again paused dramatically and repeated himself for emphasis: **"People don't buy what you do; they buy why you do it."**

He then paused again and a smile came to his face.

He pointed to the disruptive rock star and said, "Let me give you an example using this guy right here. Now, full disclosure, I can be a judgmental prick sometimes. So when this guy walked into the room with his pink, sequined flip phone, spiked hair, leather jacket and—what are those, ostrich boots?—I thought to myself, who is this disrespectful a**hole? But then something amazing happened. When he introduced himself, it was beautiful. Because while the rest of you people got up in front of the room and told everyone WHAT you did for a living, HE got up and told us WHY he did what he did. And you know what? He got me, and I get him! So I am all in! If he calls me and asks me for anything—ANYTHING—in the future, my answer will be yes. Because his why and my why are the same...and THAT, my friends, is the power of 'why.'"

This was a mic-drop moment for the room.

I learned later that the "rock star" was Bobby Sager, a venture capitalist turned philanthropist, who just happens to hang out with real rock stars.

According to Sting, his rock star friend and travel mate, Bobby is "a big brash guy from Boston...an old Nepal hand, flamboyant, eccentric, inexhaustible world traveler and practical philanthropist."

---

[3] I ran into Dr. Tom this year. He doesn't talk about spines anymore. Instead, he talks about their purpose. "We Make Lives Better" is now backed by dozens of his favorite stories.

The company presidents of the world apparently agree with the lead singer of the Police. In 2013, I was in Istanbul to see Sager receive the Hickok Award from YPO. This, the highest honor given to a member, was the result of Bobby living his purpose: "Hands-on, eyeball-to-eyeball philanthropy."

As Bobby told our YPO group that day, he believes that for philanthropy to work, the philanthropist, the person giving, must become the real "currency"; that only by contributing your time, energy and unique talents, along with your checkbook, can you maximize the return on investment you get from philanthropy.

Sure, he was a multimillionaire. Yes, his living room floor used to be the basketball court from the Boston Garden. Big whip. What he really cared about was his purpose.

WHY CONSCIOUS CAPITALISM COULD SAVE THE WORLD

Christina, Bobby and Simon all point to a superhero power shared by many Disruptors: They are conscious capitalists; they put a higher purpose ahead of profits; they start with "why."

Conscious capitalism has been gaining popularity among millennials. You may notice, for example, that sock companies are selling and giving away socks. Buy a pair, and they will donate a pair to someone in need. Shoe companies are selling and giving away shoes, and beer companies are providing clean water for impoverished communities. These are all a result of leaders who are purpose driven.

I am also now a convert. But it took a while.

Even though my friend Rajendra (Raj) Sisodia is the co-author (with John Mackey, CEO of Whole Foods) of the best-seller "Conscious Capitalism," I was skeptical of their thinking for the longest time.

However, I can no longer ignore the headlines and impact that companies are having on the world. So while I used to think that all capitalists were naturally "conscious," I was being nearsighted. I was wrong.

Before I get into how my mind was changed—and raise the blood pressure of some of you—let's make sure we are starting on the same page.

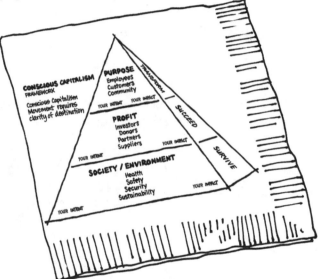

The term "conscious capitalism" is used to describe businesses that serve the interests of *all* of what its advocates argue are the major stakeholders of every company: communities, customers, employees, the environment, suppliers—and investors.

Leaders who embrace conscious capitalism will tell you that by keeping *all* of those stakeholders in mind, it allows them to focus on a higher purpose than simply making a profit.

So what *was* my problem with the concept? It might have been the same as yours.

As a lifelong entrepreneur with roots in branding, I scoffed at the phrase itself "conscious capitalism." I mean, come on! Does that mean I have been unconsciously at the wheel if I wasn't part of this enlightened tribe? All business people are consciously at work trying to achieve some outcome—usually profits. And as a capitalist for even longer than I have been an entrepreneur, I think profits are a good thing.[4]

What I was missing is that most leaders are very selective when it comes to the stakeholders they choose to serve, and this limits their global impact and, surprisingly, their profits.

When I talked to Raj about my "I-don't-get-it" reaction, he responded with data. His research shows that brands following the principles of conscious capitalism returned 1,025 percent during his decade-long study. The S&P 500 yielded 316 percent during the same time. In other words, conscious capitalism companies did more than three times as well.

But according to Raj, there are more important benefits of conscious capitalism than financial return. For example, they have:

- Higher trust among stakeholders.
- A deeper customer understanding (I believe this is THE key to innovation).
- Leaner teams that focus on value creation instead of depending on management to do it.
- High employee engagement.
- Extremely low levels of employee turnover.

---

[4] My accountant would beg to differ.

All of these are signs of a company—and its people—being "on purpose."

Fair enough. But it was only recently that I've started to see—and believe—in the real power of conscious capitalism.

First, I came to understand that focusing only on profits comes at a high cost.

- If you focus only on selling more donuts, the cost may be obesity and heart disease.
- If you focus only on selling more booze, the cost may be addiction and broken families.
- If you focus only on selling more guns, the cost may be dead kids.

Now, if I sold donuts, booze or guns for a living, you can bet that I'd have conjured up a well-articulated argument, which would include words and phrases like: indulgence, moderation, freedom of choice and the second amendment.

But to deny that there is a direct, causal relationship between muffins and muffin tops is silly. I am what I eat.[5]

Enter the conscious business leaders.

They move past deniability and into action. They take a stand and responsibility for unwanted and unintended outcomes. They choose purpose over only profits. And in doing so, they demonstrate the leadership many of us long for in our governments.

---

[5] Stop staring at my muffin top.

Keep in mind that Christina did not leave the collection industry; she chose to stay and change it. She made a conscious decision to serve all of her stakeholders, which (miraculously) resulted in higher profits and all kinds of other goodness.

The impact is now moving beyond business. Conscious business leaders are now taking on purposeful, society-shifting actions once reserved for governments. Conscious leaders are quite literally helping their constituents vote with their pocketbooks.

Here's an example. In December 2017, the U.S. government removed two million acres from Utah's national monuments, potentially opening hundreds of thousands of them to drilling, mining and grazing.

Much to the dismay of environmentalists, *The Salt Lake Tribune* reported, it appeared, that Interior Secretary Ryan Zinke was taking the side of the coal, gas and cattle industries instead of the environment.

But in the age of social media, it quickly became apparent that a couple of conscious companies would try to change that.

Outdoor outfitter Patagonia posted this pop-up message on their website:

"The president stole your land. In an illegal move, the president just reduced the size of Bears Ears and Grand Staircase-Escalante National Monuments. This is the largest elimination of protected land in American history."

When I read the message, I immediately went to Patagonia.com and did my Christmas shopping. Why? Because I was so impressed that a company would risk sales to stand up for what I believe in that I wanted to support them. Many of my friends did the same.

A similar response came after the government's inaction following the Parkland, Florida, school shootings in 2018. Dick's Sporting Goods, followed by Walmart, followed by Kroger (some of its Fred Meyer stores sell guns in Alaska, Idaho, Oregon and Washington) all took steps to change their own "laws" related to gun sales.

And it didn't end there. REI announced that it had suspended contracts with Vista Outdoor, maker of, among other things, CamelBak water bottles, Bell bicycle helmets and Giro ski goggles.

Why? Because Vista Outdoor also has brands that make guns and ammunition.

Here's what REI said about their decision.

"REI does not sell guns. We believe that it is the job of companies that manufacture and sell guns and ammunition to work towards common sense solutions that prevent the type of violence that happened in Florida last month. We have decided to place a hold on future orders of products that Vista sells through REI while we assess how Vista proceeds. Companies are showing they can contribute if they are willing to lead. We encourage Vista to do just that."

But being a conscious business can come at a price. Delta Airlines has been "punished" by the state of Georgia for deciding to no longer offer NRA members discounts. The state eliminated a tax subsidy worth an estimated $20 million to the company.

Upon hearing this, I wondered if less (or more) people would be flying Delta, or if Delta was considering moving its 30,000 employees out of Georgia.

Or if Amazon decided to remove Atlanta from its short list of 20 cities (narrowed from 238) for its new $5 billion facility that will create 50,000 jobs. (Virginia and New York won in a tie.)

Being a leader comes with responsibility. What do you want to be responsible for?

YOUR PURPOSE TRUMPS EVERYTHING

A mentor once told me that if you want to understand what a person really cares about, look at his calendar and his checkbook. This is really a great way to measure if a person is working "on purpose."

Justin Abernathy is a serial entrepreneur who works on purpose. His purpose is "to lift others while climbing." To Justin, this means striving to learn, grow and become more expert in his personal and business life—and help others do the same along the way. I've personally witnessed how this purpose manifests itself in his personal and professional life.

> If you are searching for your purpose, your checkbook and calendar provide valuable clues about what you really (REALLY) care about the most.

I'll tell you more about that in a moment. But first, a quick life lesson that Justin taught me: Never, ever, EVER make an important decision after drinking four beers. I learned this lesson nine months after drinking—you guessed it—four beers.

In the middle of a party celebrating the 13th-year gathering of an entrepreneurial group, Justin and his brother Jason approached me and about 25 of their other entrepreneurial buddies and asked us if we were tough enough to compete in a triathlon—more specifically, a half Ironman. Like many of you, I had no idea what a half Ironman was, when (after just finishing my fourth beer) I boldly declared, "I AM IN!" Many of my fellow entrepreneurs around the table were equally naïve when they made the same declaration.[6]

I now know that a half Ironman consists of a 1.5-mile swim, followed by a 54-mile bike ride, followed by a 13-mile run (or in my case, pitiful crawl).

When I sobered up and realized I'd made a stupid commitment, I came up with three simple goals: show up, finish and survive.[7]

It was during the race that I saw Justin and Jason living their purpose during their personal lives. About two miles into the final leg of the triathlon, Justin and his brother Jason—both extreme athletes and Ironmen—walked with me for miles. They could see that I was exhausted and suffering but still determined. Since they had finished long before me, they could have been relaxing and celebrating a great race. But instead, they chose to encourage me and help me finish. I can still hear and feel their encouragement today.

Three years later, I saw Jason go back into the water during a swim to make sure another friend, who was terrified, got through the first leg.

An even better example of living his purpose happened after hurricane Maria devastated the Caribbean. Justin and Jason had moved their business to Puerto Rico. In 2017, hurricane Maria plowed through the island, leaving their neighbors desperate for water, food, medicine and power. Although the Abernathy brothers could have easily headed back to the mainland U.S., where they had other offices, they instead decided to lift others. Together, with their friend John Ratliff, they orchestrated and financed more than 30 private flights with goods and services from the mainland. At one point, Justin (a technology entrepreneur) found himself riding in

---

[6] Some of them had (substantially) more than four beers.
[7] I had stopped swimming after that uncomfortable co-ed Speedo incident during my freshman year in high school.

the back of a pickup truck with a shotgun in his hands, making sure he could get food and medicine to his inland neighbors.

Justin will tell you these were some of the toughest—and best—days of his life. He was living his purpose. Just check his calendar and his checkbook.

DISRUPTOR TAKEAWAYS AND HACKS

1. **Your purpose may make people angry.** Disruptors often pursue a purpose that is antithetical to an industry. Christina Harbridge focused on being "nice" in an industry that made its money by being mean. Once you find your purpose, consider applying it to an industry where it will be most disruptive.

2. **Creating the best product or service is not a purpose.** Do not confuse what you make or how you make it with WHY you make it.

3. **People buy purpose first, product second.** Patagonia gear costs more than their competitors' products. But their customers are so aligned with the company's purpose of living as one with nature and the environment that product cost becomes less important.

4. **Your purpose will sometimes defy the laws of business.** Patagonia encourages people NOT to buy their products. Instead, they want people to repair and reuse items.

5. **Reward the purpose.** How are you measuring success? Look for key performance metrics that tie directly to your company's purpose. For example, if you are all about less plastic in the ocean, reward ideas that result in X number of tons of plastic removed from waterways instead of things like awareness of plastic pollution.

DISRUPTOR TAKEAWAYS AND HACKS (cont.)

6. **The (young) world is watching.** Millennials will often work longer, harder and for less money if the purpose of a company aligns with their values. Additionally, they are more and more likely to reject a product or service if it conflicts with what matters most to them.

7. **Success or significance?** Watch a successful person as they approach their later years and they will say things like: "I've made my money. Now I want to make a difference. I am focused on my legacy." Here's an idea: Why not start with the end in mind and move backward?

8. **Purpose is the ultimate economic engine.** Governments used to be relied upon to keep good and evil In check. Today, it is our business leaders who have the most leverage to make the world a better place. Since we live in a global economy, this is now a global responsibility. It is our job to take this responsibility to heart and make a difference.

(Treasure hunt! What's your purpose?
  List the times when you feel most alive.)

Chapter 10
Walt Disney's Secret

How do you create a billion-dollar company? In the case of the company we are about to talk about, it began in an unlikely place.

John and Ellen met at a high school graduation party the summer before they both headed off to college. It wasn't exactly love at first sight. But as you will see, their differences drew them together.

John came off as a bit too intense for Ellen. Even then he was a hard-driving, fierce competitor. He was the son of a high school shop teacher who taught him to value hard work and about getting his hands dirty and winning. He wasn't going to let anything get in his way.

But Ellen wasn't put off by John's intensity, and after their second or third date, she noticed he kind of reminded her of her dad—an intense but thoughtful gentleman whose professional career included being a Navy captain and operating manufacturing facilities for Keebler. Ellen had grown up watching her father run a "tight ship," always planning and making sure small details were attended to and the people around him were well-cared for. He had dreams but always wanted to have a well-thought-out plan in place before taking the leap. John seemed wired the same way.

When John met Ellen, he thought she was a little nuts. Sure, she was strategic, but in a big-picture way. She trusted her gut and didn't let details slow her down. Ellen was comfortable jumping quickly into action and figuring things out along the way. In addition, John noticed that Ellen pushed him to take risks. He liked that.

Their romance lasted through that first summer after their high school senior year, and since they were going to different colleges, they made the wise decision to work through the "long-distance college relationship" phase by not being exclusive. They dated off and on through college, making the most of their times together during holidays and summers.

Bucking the odds, their relationship grew stronger over time and distance. They were married in 1994—seven years after meeting—proving that opposites really do attract.

In the spring of 1995, the newlyweds decided to move to Seattle. Or more accurately, Ellen talked John into taking a leap and moving to Seattle. Ellen's dad—the Navy captain—had been raised in the area, and childhood vacations to visit his family had left their mark. Ellen had grown up dreaming of living in the Pacific Northwest. To make her dream happen, she assured John that when they got there, everything would work out fine. (Besides, if it didn't, "they could just move back to Chicago.")

John eventually agreed, figuring that since he and Ellen were highly employable and had no kids, they had very little to lose.

Leaning on his reputation for being a hard-working strategy guy, John quickly landed a job in Ernst & Young's management consulting division in Seattle. From there, his primary client—AT&T Wireless—hired him to lead their IT Architecture and Shared Services group. These folks typically handle and deliver all technical and administrative issues that the business units of a company (e.g., finance, human resources, etc.) have in common. For the first time, John experienced life on the other side of the table. He was now in a fast-growing company, buying consulting services from strategy shops like the one he had worked for in Chicago.

And perhaps, not surprisingly, John saw some things in the consulting industry that desperately needed improvement.

Meanwhile, Ellen decided to try her hand at real estate, helping relocate fast-climbing Microsoft and AT&T executives. The market was booming and Ellen's straight-talking, hardworking, Midwestern approach put people at ease. Her boss told her that she had a way of making clients imagine what was next for their families that was absolutely inspiring! Before too long, she was crushing it.

Life was good. The plan had worked, and John and Ellen were living the dream in Seattle.

And this is where our story repeats itself.

In 2001, John met a headhunter from Two Degrees, an accounting staffing firm. In the course of a conversation that went really well, John told the headhunter, Troy Johnson, that someday he'd like to open his own consulting company. He had learned so much and had some strong opinions about how consulting was bought and sold. Troy immediately connected John to his boss Brad Jackson, who also wanted to create a technology consulting division within his company Two Degrees.

As an entrepreneur, Brad saw how Microsoft and other technology firms in the area had created more problems to solve than there were people to solve them.

John and Brad immediately hit it off. Brad saw John as someone who could execute his vision, and John saw this as the entrepreneurial opportunity he'd been seeking.

Most important, just like his relationship with Ellen, John noticed that he and Brad had values that were similar and individual strengths that seemed to complement the other's weaknesses. Brad was big picture; John was about the details. Brad had an idea a minute; John wanted to work through the most important idea first. Brad enjoyed imagining the future; John loved making plans to get there. You get the idea.

Once again, opposites attract.

Not surprisingly, Brad (the risk-taker) loved the idea of starting a consulting practice—and so did Ellen, who encouraged John to jump in and help Brad with this adventure. She believed in the idea—and John. Besides her success, selling homes gave them some runway.

This story has gone on long enough, and you probably sense where it is heading.

Today, John and Brad (and co-founder and connector Troy Johnson) have more than 5,500 employees and over $1 billion in revenue. Their consulting company, Slalom, has been named one of *Fortune's* 100 Best Companies to Work For. Along the way, Brad was named to Glassdoor's Top CEO list, and John was named Ernst & Young's Entrepreneur of the Year, ironically, for creating the kind of company he always wished Ernst & Young was when he worked there.

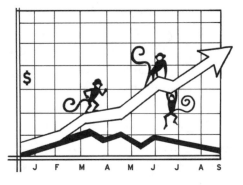

Meanwhile, Ellen used her growing expertise in the real estate market to upgrade their home three times for their three kids and two dogs.

All of this was made possible because three special and wildly different people managed to find the yin for their yang.

One (John Tobin) was even good enough to marry my kid sister.[1]

THERE ARE AT LEAST TWO KINDS OF CRAZY

"You. Complete. Me."
— Tom Cruise as Jerry McGuire
to his girlfriend.

Do you have a lot of crazy ideas? Or do you work with a boss or business partner who loves to come up with the next big thing?

---

[1] Please, nobody tell John I said that. We wouldn't want him to get a big head.

Or...are you relentless when it comes to focusing on the details of a strategy or creating a process and metrics to make sure plans are executed with precision?

I call these two types of personalities the Idea Monkey and the Ringleader. When things go well, each ends up in a job that appeals to his or her passion. The Idea Monkey uses his creative energy to become a designer, a strategist or even a CEO. The Ringleader may be an engineer, a financial expert, COO or CEO. Regardless, they advance to drive companies in completely different ways.

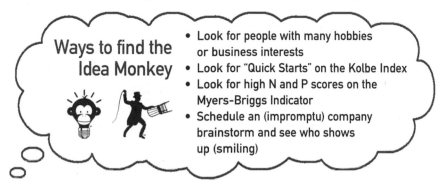

Ways to find the Idea Monkey

- Look for people with many hobbies or business interests
- Look for "Quick Starts" on the Kolbe Index
- Look for high N and P scores on the Myers-Briggs Indicator
- Schedule an (impromptu) company brainstorm and see who shows up (smiling)

The Idea Monkeys are big picture, divergent thinkers who can connect lots of seemingly unrelated ideas (often hundreds of ideas). They are risk-takers, multitaskers and imaginative. They often believe that anything is possible, and they set off to solve complicated challenges with their disruptive insights and ideas.

Ringleaders care deeply about the details. They prefer to have a well-articulated plan before moving forward. They focus on the essential, not the important, wanting to work on the few projects that really matter. They are not impressed with platitudes about amazing futures. Instead, they want to see how the numbers work, believing that what gets measured gets done.

As is always the case, your strength is also your weakness. And so it is with Idea Monkeys and Ringleaders.

Left on their own, Idea Monkeys will start too many projects at once. Since they have not worked through the details, they may run out of time, money or friends before their (fantastical) dreams are realized.

A third of entrepreneurs are out of business in less than two years. Most entrepreneurs are Idea Monkeys.

Are you a Walt or a Roy?
Either answer is great, as long as you know what makes you feel strong.

Ringleaders have exactly the opposite challenge. Playing it safe, they will often make a proven product or service only marginally better. Small differences don't command the attention of the market and won't support higher margins. Or they will move too conservatively and slowly, taking too long to respond to an impatient market. They ruin good with perfect.

The Kolbe test (Kolbe.com) is a great way to get some clues about which way you and your team learn and act. The results of the Kolbe test points to the natural strengths of a person across four different areas: Fact Finder, Follow Thru, Quick Start and Implementer. To keep it really simple, I've found that Idea Monkeys tend to be high "Quick Starts" on the Kolbe Index, while Ringleaders have higher Fact Finder and Follow Thru scores.

When these skills are matched and in balance (i.e., when Idea Monkeys and Ringleaders are working together in harmony), beautiful things happen. The world changes for the better.

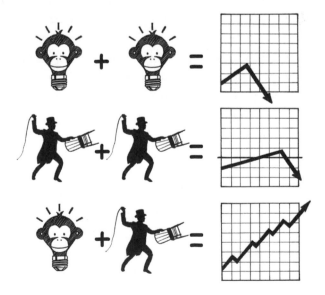

The Wright brothers are a great example. Nobody was more surprised by the successful invention of flight than their parents, who spent sleepless nights worrying about their youngest son, Orville. He was the class clown, a truant and basically a horrible student. He spent his time daydreaming, not studying. And his parents and teachers were flummoxed. He was nothing like his older brother, Wilbur.

Wilbur, who was four years older, was the good son. Like many first-born children, he followed the rules, got straight A's and diligently went about the business of making his younger brother look like a complete loser.[2]

Wilbur was the complete package. He lettered in four different sports, and his grades and diligence paid off when he received a full scholarship to Yale.

You can almost see Orville—the high school dropout—rolling his eyes.[3]

Luckily for Orville (and all of us), Wilbur played hockey. During Wilbur's senior year, he took a puck to the face, which knocked out all of his front teeth, leaving the handsome young man…not so handsome. Wilbur was so embarrassed at how he looked that he elected NOT to go to Yale and instead stayed home and helped his younger brother with entrepreneurship—first in a printing business and next in a bicycle repair shop.

This twist of fate saved his younger brother's life. Here's how.

Orville was a dreamer who wanted to fly and was literally willing to risk his life every time he had inspiration about how to make that happen. But each time Orville was ready to take off, his older brother—the diligent, rule-following, good son—would recommend that Orville's theories be tested and more experiments be done.

---

[2] Yes, I have an older brother.
[3] Yes, I am projecting.

Because of this balance between bold vision and thoughtful experimentation, the Wright brothers eventually flew successfully.

Companies that have created an intentional balance between these two types of personalities win, while those that are dramatically out of balance lose. It's as simple as that.

HOW TO WIN

"Culture eats strategy for breakfast."
– Michael Porter, Harvard Business School professor

They are out of balance. This was the first thought that popped into my mind when I read Steve Blank's *Harvard Business Review* article explaining why Jeff Immelt lost his job as CEO of GE in 2017. Steve argued that activist investors forced out Immelt because of the long, languishing performance of the company's stock. As an innovation consultant, I have learned that when growth and profits have stalled, it usually means a company's leadership is out of balance.

The second thing I thought was that a bunch of irritated Ringleaders had lost their patience and taken control of the company because following Mr. Immelt out the door was vice chair, innovation lead, force of nature and Idea Monkey Beth Comstock. This move made GE even more out of balance and, to me, signaled likely short-term gains and a critical threat to long-term survival.

I'll never forget the meeting that Beth asked me to attend at GE headquarters. I was brought in to give a presentation to her leadership team about how large firms balance the tension between the visionaries and the operators; between the Walt and Roy Disneys of the world; the BFAs and the MBAs; the Jeff Immelts and the Jack Welches; the Idea Monkeys and the Ringleaders.

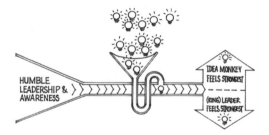

As I recall, half of the room was on the edge of their seats during my talk. The other half was too worried about their day jobs to pay attention. After all, they had jobs to do; they were supposed to be making money today, not thinking about the future.

The week before the meeting, I had two conflicting conversations. One senior GE executive whispered in my ear that it had been 13 years since the company launched a product, service or business based on one of their thousands of patents. He thought they desperately needed help figuring out how to reignite the entrepreneurial, inventive spirit that had created the company.

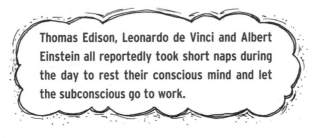

Thomas Edison, Leonardo de Vinci and Albert Einstein all reportedly took short naps during the day to rest their conscious mind and let the subconscious go to work.

I didn't know if he was correct, but I did know that GE was started by Thomas Edison—one of the greatest inventors in history. So the conversation surprised me. It also made me sad.

The second conversation was with a very senior engineer and operator named Nabil[4]. He suggested—quite strongly—that I make my presentation completely about a data-driven process. In a thick, Indian accent, he begged me to "tell us what to measure, when to

---

[4] I changed his name because I don't want to be a jerk. I changed it to Nabil because I don't think I know anyone with this name. If I am wrong, then his name was Chuck.

measure it and how to measure it. We are all about process. Nothing else matters. Nothing."

About halfway through my presentation, I noticed that Nabil was sitting to my right, contorting his body into the shape of a pretzel. He was in the middle of realizing that I had elected to speak about design thinking rather than data measurement. My talk appeared to be making him physically ill. Where—he seemed to be wondering—was Six Sigma when you need it?

Now, years later, I am afraid that at GE, innovation has become a four-letter word. This is an all-too-familiar outcome in conservative, historically profitable companies dominated by Ringleaders.

Under Immelt and Comstock's leadership, GE was committed to innovation and redefining the company's place in the future. They were trying to move GE from a product company to becoming a platform for new products, services and business models. They were seeking to strike a balance between short-term profits and long-term growth.

After the meeting, I was asked to join their innovation advisory board, and my company and others were hired to help create and implement systems that leveraged the principles of design thinking and lean startup throughout the organization.

GE needed to get back to its entrepreneurial roots because some believed that Thomas Edison's company had forgotten how to innovate. They believed that Ringleader operators like former CEO

Jack Welch had done such a good job eliminating mistakes that the company had lost its ability to take risks and experiment. Immelt was committed to taking on this issue. Immelt is now gone.

To be fair, he had 16 years to move the needle, and he only started working on innovation in earnest during the second half of his tenure. It is also fair to ask why companies like mine did not push his team harder or have a more immediate impact on stock valuation. We worked with Beth and her team for about a year and saw first-hand the massive challenge that leadership at GE was taking on.

It's a challenge you might recognize.

For large, publicly traded companies, the central question was then—and is today—how do you ensure profit while you are experimenting with new business and service models? If you are an Idea Monkey like Edison or Jeff Immelt, the answer is to out-innovate your competition. If you are a Ringleader like GE's former CEO Jack Welch or Walt Disney's brother Roy, the answer is to find new—albeit creative—ways to cut costs, tighten distribution and optimize your current operations.

Idea Monkeys	Ringleaders
Diverge	Converge
Predict it	Prove it
Ideas, ideas, ideas!	Process, process, process
3-3-9-3 Kolbe Quick Start	8-8-3-3 Kolbe Fact Finder, Follow Thru
Ready, fire, aim	Plan and execute with precision
Anything is possible	Let's make sure it is possible
Energy, sparkle fingers, cheerleader	Stay calm, stay focused, stay the course

For Welch, this meant institutionalizing programs like Six Sigma to minimize costly mistakes. The focus clearly paid off. During Welch's two-decade tenure, the company became the most valuable in the world in terms of stock valuation. The company went from a market value of $14 billion, the 10th highest in the world when he took over as CEO, to more than $410 billion at the time of his retirement in 2001.

For Immelt, it meant institutionalizing design thinking and lean innovation management to help identify more elegant futures. It meant acquiring and investing in young startups. It meant working to instill a culture of innovation.

Right now, disruptive startups are putting a lot of pressure on incumbent leaders like GE. Under pressure of disruption, each archetype—the Idea Monkey and the Ringleader—respond in opposite ways.

The Idea Monkey wants to envision new models, and the Ringleader wants to make the old model work better.

In my experience, neither reaction is appropriate. Rather, a balanced response—one that invests in the future while optimizing the present—is what works best.

But this balance is ridiculously difficult to strike—particularly when you have impatient shareholders.

Bob Cancalosi worked at GE for 31 years. For the last seven, he was GE's director of global customer leadership education.

Bob introduced me to the term "ambidextrous leadership." His answer to the most common question he got from his customers was: "How can I focus on running a business effectively today while always preparing it for tomorrow?"

His answer? "You must listen to customers and deeply understand their pain points, and then you can position current solutions and co-create future solutions. The moment you stop listening, you are finished. Too many large corporations lose this ability to listen because they are focused on near-term results.

"It can be devastating when there is so much focus on the 'now' that it prevents the appropriate investment in the 'next.' Thinking about tomorrow while working on today is an ambidextrous leadership challenge. The best leaders know how to listen, and at his best, this was Jeff Immelt's superhero power."

In 1987, the movie "Wall Street" featured actor Michael Douglas as Gordon Gekko, a corporate raider who famously said, "Greed is good." Today, corporate raiders like Gekko have been rebranded as "activist investors," but the message is still the same. And GE's activist shareholders have now had their way with the company, which includes helping to install a new CEO.

Newsflash: Jack is back, at least in spirit. I suspect that GE's new CEO, John Flannery, will make dramatic and difficult decisions to create near-term financial results. In the process, I suspect he will tilt GE further out of balance.[5]

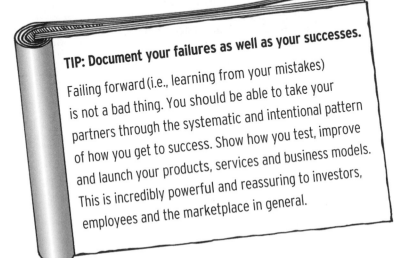

TIP: Document your failures as well as your successes.

Failing forward (i.e., learning from your mistakes) is not a bad thing. You should be able to take your partners through the systematic and intentional pattern of how you get to success. Show how you test, improve and launch your products, services and business models. This is incredibly powerful and reassuring to investors, employees and the marketplace in general.

---

[5] It didn't take long. Two months after I wrote this sentence, GE was replaced by Walgreens on the *Fortune* 500 list. Shortly thereafter, Flannery was replaced by a new CEO.

In the past, shareholders tended to love executives like Jack Welch and cringed at the ideas of visionary leaders. This is because shareholders naturally care about increasing stock price today, and innovation programs are investments in the tomorrow that decrease short-term profits. So to shareholders, innovation can seem like a waste of time and money.

But things are changing. Becoming a billion-dollar company can now happen almost overnight. This accelerated rate of change is not lost on executives of *Fortune* 500 companies. For example, while it used to take companies generations to reach a $1 billion valuation, Facebook did it in seven years. It took Uber five years and the crypto startup Telegram four months.

Facebook, Uber and Telegram were not started by a Ringleader, but you can be damn sure that they eventually will be run by one.

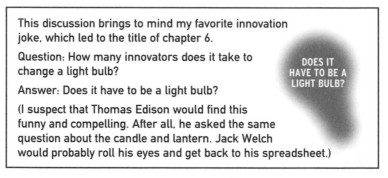

This discussion brings to mind my favorite innovation joke, which led to the title of chapter 6.

Question: How many innovators does it take to change a light bulb?

Answer: Does it have to be a light bulb?

(I suspect that Thomas Edison would find this funny and compelling. After all, he asked the same question about the candle and lantern. Jack Welch would probably roll his eyes and get back to his spreadsheet.)

DOES IT HAVE TO BE A LIGHT BULB?

We've seen this movie before: Impatient shareholders get a visionary leader fired and replace him with an operator who cuts costs, departments and dismantles the systems designed to address the future of the company. The focus is on short-term profits and appeasing shareholders.

How does this work out in the long run? Just ask Sears investors.

In 1989, Sears—founded 106 years before—was America's biggest retailer. Today, Sears, the original "buy anything" company, is now reportedly teetering on the edge of extinction. You can argue that they are being replaced by a new version of themselves—a young "catalog" company called Amazon.

Sears had every right to be Amazon. Their shareholders and Ringleaders just wouldn't let them.

As Sears' management was listening to shareholders, they forgot to listen to their customers. I wonder how Sears' stockholders are feeling today?

Where are Thomas Edison, Walt Disney and Richard Warren Sears when you need them?

THERE IS GOOD NEWS

All of this brings me to the good news. Private companies have an unfair competitive advantage when it comes to innovation: Their owners often have a long-term outlook that allows them to invest in the future.

Here's an example.

My wife and I had the honor of having lunch with Jim Liautaud. (I'll give you his background in a minute.) We were in California for a business event when Jim shared a story that I will never forget. Jim got an emotional call from his son Jimmy in 1983. Jimmy was a freshman at Eastern Illinois University. According to Jim, the call went something like this:

"Dad, I suck at school. I've always sucked at school. I hate school. Why am I at school?"

Jim told us his response was an immediate "Well, f**k it son! What do you want to do?"

Jimmy's response was that he wanted to start a sandwich shop—one that would compete with McDonald's, Subway, Burger King....

Now, as a father of two sons myself, I would have likely told my kids they were nuts. Like most dads, I suspect I would have told my boy to finish school and start a business when he was better prepared.

Jim did just the opposite. Jim said, "Sounds good to me," and asked his son if he was open to a little help.

Jimmy went on to start his sandwich shop, but before I tell you how it turned out, I want to tell you a bit more about his dad, Jim. Jim Liautaud was an industrialist and inventor. He started and ran five businesses before the age of 50. Much of his business success was due to his 50+ inventions, including a patent for a molding process used to help manufacture the first airbag.

... and behind each one of these talents should be a committed Ringleader ensuring laser focus and that only the best ideas survive.

Jim knew a few things about business. So when Jim asked his son if he was open to a little help, it meant more than just supporting him financially. It meant helping him with business plans and processes. It meant focusing on the right things at the right time. It meant giving Jimmy the space to do what he loved to do and did the best.

Today, Jimmy John's sells more than $2 billion worth of sandwiches a year. You don't sell that many sandwiches unless you measure tomato slices and just about everything else—which they do. But more important, you don't sell $2.5 billion worth of sandwiches unless a Ringleader father loves his Idea Monkey son.

Who completes you? Who is your business soul mate?

SCALING TOGETHER

By now, I hope you can see that Disruptors can take the shape of Idea Monkeys or Ringleaders. Idea Monkeys tend to disrupt with completely new ways of thinking about a challenge, while Ringleaders tend to lean into process and measurement to solve it in a proven, reliable way, improving a bit what has come before. For example, A.G. Lafley twice helped accelerate growth at consumer goods maker Procter & Gamble by changing their processes. And Sheryl Sandberg has navigated Facebook through incredible growth with her operational genius.[6]

Over time, companies begin to become a reflection of their leaders. And usually, in very successful companies, this means too many Ringleaders. (As I said earlier, most companies will eventually be run by Ringleaders.) The reason for this can be summed up in one word: scaling. Once a visionary Disruptor has created a completely new product, service, business model or platform, it is time for scaling. Processes, systems and measurements must be implemented and improved so the idea can go from a few customers to many. This is what Ringleaders do best. This is also what Idea Monkeys do the worst (they have moved on to their next big idea). So, over time, a very successful company is made up of way more Ringleaders than Idea Monkeys. That's how it scaled successfully.

---

[6] Take it from an Idea Monkey: Ideas are easy; execution, not so much.

In the beginning of this book, I talked about how the future was coming faster and faster. Gone are the days when one great idea would last you 50 or even 10 years. Successful companies in the future will be the ones able to reinvent themselves WHILE scaling. Disruptive Idea Monkeys and Ringleaders must find a way to make this happen—together.

THE INNOVATION PARADOX

When it comes to Ringleaders and Idea Monkeys scaling a company together, I have some good news and some bad news. The good news is that there is a proven, reliable process to make it happen. And that is good news because Ringleaders love process, so there is hope.

The bad news is what I call the "innovation paradox."

In 2011, my partners and I wrote a book titled "Brand New: Solving the Innovation Paradox." It outlined a process designed to solve the fundamental challenge of corporate (Read: large, established) companies when it comes to innovation: The harder we try to innovate, the worse we get at innovation. This is what we call the innovation paradox.

Here's how the idea came about. For years, we saw intelligent, charismatic and committed CEOs investing millions to create more innovative cultures, only to be seemingly worse off years later. We asked ourselves, "Could what we are seeing actually be right? The more the company spent on innovation, the worse they got at it?"

We researched our observation to see if we were on to something. We asked more than 800 leaders who were in charge of the innovation initiatives within their organizations a series of questions. You will see them in a moment, and we found out we were right.

But it gets worse.

In 2016, the consulting firm Accenture did similar research about innovation, and their study contained the same questions we asked four years earlier.

The reason the Accenture study is important is because it was conducted after "innovation" had become a buzzword. So many companies were trying to figure out how to create company cultures that could quickly respond to the future that virtually every consulting and creative services firm jumped into the game. And yet, despite the effort, attention and capital investments, the same executives doing the work admitted that they had gotten approximately 20 percent worse at doing it.

The innovation paradox had grown more dramatic, as you can see from the data below.

Executives' Beliefs	2012	2016[7]
Innovation is critical to our strategy	67%	84%
We are missing opportunities to exploit	53%	72%
We don't learn from past mistakes	36%	60%
We are risk averse	53%	72%

Ouch.

---

[7] Yes, if you are a chief innovation officer, you probably should be depressed.

THE JUNK DRAWER

My grandfather had a junk drawer. As a kid, I loved to explore it. It was full of tools, hardware, screws…virtually anything you would need to fix anything. And as a product of the great recession, my grandfather believed in fixing everything.

There was only one issue: He liked glue too much. Judging by the furniture, mugs, toys and sports gear that had been glued, reglued and glued yet again, for my grandpa, there wasn't any problem that could not be fixed with glue. Although his junk drawer was full of other useful tools, he always reached for the glue.

So, too, is it with innovation efforts. Leaders always seem to reach for their own version of glue. And as useful as their tool of choice may be in certain situations, it is suboptimal or even destructive when applied inappropriately.

When it comes to innovation tools, you want to be like a master mechanic. You need to have a garage full of well-tested, reliable tools, AND you need to know when, where and who should apply them.

SOLVING THE INNOVATION PARADOX

I promised you good news, and at this point, you could probably use some.

Earlier in this chapter, I pointed out how Ringleaders prefer convergence while Idea Monkeys are all about divergence. When these opposing preferences meet, they can create either destructive drama or sustainable industry disruption.

To create the more desirable of these two, you must rely on process — a process that informs your team what tools to use and when to use them.

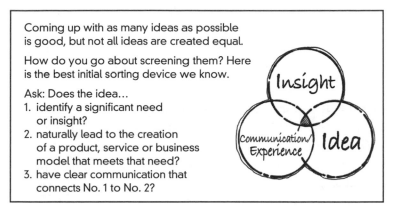

Coming up with as many ideas as possible is good, but not all ideas are created equal.

How do you go about screening them? Here is the best initial sorting device we know.

Ask: Does the idea...
1. identify a significant need or insight?
2. naturally lead to the creation of a product, service or business model that meets that need?
3. have clear communication that connects No. 1 to No. 2?

Insight

Communication/ Experience   Idea

The innovation process is a masterfully choreographed dance between time-tested divergent and convergent practices. This balance between reimagining and reengineering makes everyone feel strong and accelerates the best ideas to market.

As you move through the innovation process, every divergent activity has an equally important and balancing convergent activity. This allows both the Ringleaders and Idea Monkeys to complement each other's thinking and, when done well, accelerate the best thinking to market.

Idea Monkeys	Ringleaders
Brainstorm	Insight ranking
Rapid prototype	Conjoint analysis
Ethnographies	Segmentation
Innovation cafés	Culture dashboards
Open innovation	Outside subject experts
Lots of ideas	Balanced portfolio model

The best way I know to illustrate this idea is by starting with one of the Idea Monkey's favorite activities: brainstorming. This activity typically drives the Ringleader nuts because it is completely divergent—the goal being to come up with as many breakthrough ideas as possible. This, of course, distracts the Ringleader from doing "real" work like fine-tuning the current business model.

In a highly functioning organization, the Ringleader will ask the question: "Brainstorm about what?"

In a highly functioning organization, there is a process through which to answer this question quantitatively (Ringleaders love quantitative answers) and with great confidence.

We take our clients through the following formulaic process in which we construct, measure and select problems to be solved. We call these problems insights.

The process empowers the Ringleader to go to his favorite Idea Monkey and say, "Here is a specific challenge we need to solve. If we can do so, there is a billion-dollar market opportunity that we have the right to own. I need the team's best ideas to solve this problem."

When Idea Monkeys focus on solving really big, really important problems, billion-dollar ideas happen.

Here's how the formula works.

I (statement of fact) because (reason to believe), but (market tension).

Process

Use qualitative methods to generate as many insight statements as possible. Then use criteria to cull the list down to a dozen or so. Next, quantify the top insights to better understand and *prioritize* by market opportunity. Finally—and I do mean finally because for Idea Monkeys, this is the fun part—have your team generate solutions for only the top one to three ranked insights.

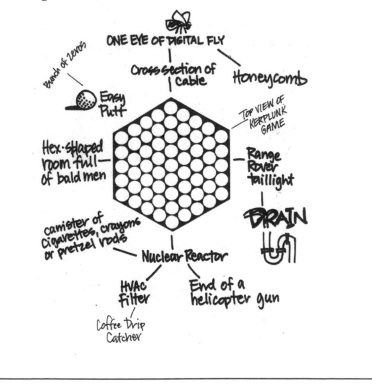

Winning Insight Example

I want my teeth to be whiter (statement of fact) because it makes me look younger (reason to believe), but brushing alone does not make my teeth white enough (market tension).

Actual billion-dollar idea: Crest Whitestrips.

Boom!

Ringleaders and Idea Monkeys have just made the world smile together.

A bonus: Some Ringleaders will have found the process above too simplistic. For them, I offer this diagram:

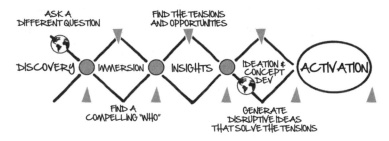

As long as you are disciplined about insights first, ideas second, you wind up in the same place.

MAKING MUSIC TOGETHER

It isn't easy to change the world or your company culture. Striking the balance between your divergent and convergent Disruptors requires more than just a process and the right tools at the right time; it requires mutual respect. The Idea Monkey and Ringleader must respect one another.

Perhaps two of the clearest examples of this yin-yang approach to creation are songwriting duos Richard Rodgers (music) and Oscar Hammerstein II (lyrics); Elton John (music) and Bernie Taupin (words).

If you talk to these duos, they will be quick to tell you that there is NOT an absolute delineation of duties all the time. The lyricists will suggest a mood/tempo ("maybe we should do it as a jazz waltz"), and the person creating the tune will suggest a phrase or maybe even the title.

There isn't resentment when this happens. They are trying to create the best song possible.

That should be your approach when you are coming with new ideas. Even though the roles of yin and yang are clearly defined, ideas should be welcome from anywhere.

When Idea Monkeys and Ringleaders move beyond a partnership to what could almost be called a brotherhood, sisterhood or even a love affair, creative masterpieces are the result. Just think: McCartney and Lennon, Jagger and Richards, Rodgers and Hammerstein... and then ask yourself again, who is the Disruptor who completes you?

DISRUPTOR TAKEAWAYS AND HACKS

1. **Balance is key.** Use tests like the Kolbe Index to make sure your team includes people who can think up the big idea (Quick Starts), people who can vet the idea (Fact Finders) and the folks who make sure it gets done (Follow Thru).

2. **Operators LOVE process.** So process frameworks are a great foundation for a culture that needs to learn how to innovate. Take care to use both divergent and convergent tools at the right time and with the right people. (Excuse the plug, but the books "Brand New" and "Free the Idea Monkey" are good reference tools for this.)

3. **Find your soul mate.** This is particularly important if you lead a company or a large team. Love and respect that their strengths complement your weaknesses.

4. **Ringleaders: Make a wish.** If you are an operator and are certain an idea is bad, swallow your pride and admit it is because you don't know how it could be done (legally, technically, financially or otherwise). Then make a wish. Instead of saying "that idea would get us all arrested," say something like "I wish we could find a way to make that idea legal." Now, sit back and watch the Idea Monkeys dance.

DISRUPTOR TAKEAWAYS AND HACKS (cont.)

5. **Idea Monkeys: Focus on insight.** As I wrote in Chapter 7, invention is coming up with an idea and then looking for someone who wants it. Innovation is starting with a significant unmet need (an insight) and then creating a compelling and unique way to solve it. Make sure you are working on only the biggest insights. This will delight the Ringleaders on your team.

6. **Put a "pivot thinker" on your team.** About five percent of the population is what we call pivot thinkers. They have the ability to toggle back and forth between great vision and great execution. These folks are rare, but they often create a great connective tissue between the extreme Idea Monkeys and Ringleaders on your team. Look for a Kolbe score like 7-7-7-3. You want Fact Finder, Follow Thru and Quick Start scores that are above 5. In a fast-paced environment, these people are priceless.

DISRUPTOR TAKEAWAYS AND HACKS (cont.)

7. Settled truths. One thing that drives Ringleaders nuts is revisiting the same topics again and again and again. Since Idea Monkeys are wired to constantly create and recreate, regardless of topic, they often don't notice when they begin to reengineer a tired issue for the umpteenth time. Ringleaders DO notice, and they view this type of behavior as a frustrating waste of time and energy.

One solution is to make a short list of "settled truths." This list, conceived together but curated by the Ringleader, should memorialize important company issues that have been fully explored, debated and resolved. For example:

Settled truth #1
We will always hire using the lens of core values first, expertise second.

Settled truth #2
We will measure growth by profits, not by revenue.

Settled truth #3
Sales is noble, and it is part of everyone's job.

You get the idea. Once you settle on a truth, it is no longer open to discussion.

DISRUPTOR TAKEAWAYS AND HACKS (cont.)

8. Beg forgiveness. Mike Moynihan runs a law firm in Chicago, so when he has "big" ideas he wants to try, he expects the cross-examination from his partners to be rigorous and tough. Over time, he's learned these debates can be taxing and time intensive, so today he avoids them completely. Instead, he jumps into action, doing a trial run to the idea, and then he brings his partners the results of his test. Says Mike, "It's like high-stakes poker. When an idea works, you should expect a few attaboys; chips you can put in the bank. I always try to have chips to play from past successful ideas. But If you run out of chips, you may find yourself in a different job."

(*You must be ready to doodle by now!*)

Chapter 11

The Art Of Being
Strategically Selfish

You jackass. That was the thought bubble above my head as I stood talking to the man beside me in the pool.

I was on a father-son retreat in Sacramento with our youngest, Cody, who was 8 years old at the time. It had been a long day of horseback riding, archery and facilitated conversation about daddy-son things like trust, love and tarantulas. I was physically and emotionally exhausted, but I was committed to spending every moment possible on the trip focused on my son.

Cody was playing tag in the pool with some other kids who didn't want parents involved, so I swam up to another dad I'd met the day before.

I asked him how his day had gone.

"It was great. I had a massage, took a nap and did some reading."

Did I mention this was a father-son retreat?

I asked him what his son was doing while he was getting his massage.[1]

He said he was horseback riding and shooting bows and arrows. "I think he had a blast. He must have. He seems super tired."

---

[1] "You self-absorbed weenie!" (Keep it in the thought bubble. Mike.)

WTF? I was immediately indignant. What kind of jackass gets a massage when he is supposed to be hanging out with his kid? Who does that kind of thing? After doing research for this book, I found out that healthy Disruptors do that sort of thing — all the time. Who knew?

THE JUDGMENT

You probably have a very successful friend who plays golf four or five times a week or a well-paid buddy who gets a massage every day. Perhaps another CEO comrade does marathons, which requires hours of training for months. Or maybe the person in the big house down the street is a triathlete, so you see her out doing crazy amounts of training on her ridiculously expensive bike and then traveling all over the world for her "hobby."

Selfish weenies, right?

Admit it. You have judged them. Just like I did to that father in the pool. You have wondered how someone could behave so selfishly while they had a family, a business, a charity or a community to attend to. You know, like you obediently do every day. Your parents clearly taught *you* right.

Divergent sidebar: My great aunt and grandmother once took me out to "dinner" (it was 2 p.m.) to convince me to get married in a Catholic church instead of the nondenominational megachurch my soon-to-be wife and I attended. They were horrified that I was straying from the faith and were bent on saving my sinful soul.

After they had a few drinks (I was abstaining because I needed to get back to work), my aunt Betsy said, "Mike, I've been going to the same church for over 40 years. I absolutely hate it, but I still go!"

Wow, compelling argument, Aunt Betsy. Not.

I now realize that while I was sitting in the pool in Sacramento, and for years after, I had been unwittingly playing the character of my aunt Betsy. I was judging behavior as unacceptable because I really didn't understand it. After all, just like Aunt Betsy, I was raised right.

PUT YOUR OWN OXYGEN MASK ON FIRST

We've all heard a flight attendant direct us to take care of ourselves before helping others in the face of an emergency. But metaphorically speaking, almost none of us actually do this. This is especially true of high-performing people with low-performing personal lives. (You know, the ones who wind up with addiction problems, three ex-spouses, hypertension, kids who don't like them, and they are 50 pounds overweight.)

One of my more vivid memories is the time when my sobbing and shrieking wife, Ruthie, threw a bottle of Ambien at me and yelled, "Will you just take these damn things?" (To Ruthie, "damn" is the pinnacle of swearing.) As I ducked and saw how upset she was, I murmured something like, "I don't need them."

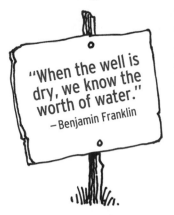

"When the well is dry, we know the worth of water."
– Benjamin Franklin

My wife was worried sick about me, and she felt helpless to make things better. At the time of the fastball Ambien pitch, I'd had weeks of sleepless nights and anxiety attacks. My doctor had prescribed the sleeping medication, suggesting that if I didn't start taking care of myself, things would go from bad to worse. I hadn't listened to him, of course, and based on Ruthie's throwing arm, things had just gone to "worse."

Ruthie saw that I wasn't taking care of myself, and she had reached her breaking point.

My oldest son had noticed too. One night when I got home from work, Ruthie handed me a letter Gunnar had written to God, asking that I get better. He was 6 years old. It broke my heart.

This story has a happy ending and a lesson for all of us who have judged our "selfish" high-performing friends.

To truly take the best care of others, we have to first take care of ourselves.

After Ruthie flung the Ambien at me, I woke up.[2] Two weeks later, I started a six-week sabbatical from work. I needed to recover from 14 years of running a business (and myself) into the ground. We went to France. I unplugged. I read, swam, went to local markets, drank wine, visited castles and ate lots of cheese. Miraculously, I lost weight. When we returned, I was revived and with a clear head, something amazing happened: The business recovered too.

---

[2] See what I did there?

Healthy Disruptors know that in order to take care of others, they must first take care of themselves. They must be mentally and physically prepared for peak performance when it is necessary.

Unhealthy Disruptors never get this message. They double down on their efforts to impact lives and often ruin their own lives in the process.

I've learned to respect and encourage the golf, the massages, the reading time, the yoga...because the leaders I see who are committed to these activities have by and large healthier companies and often healthier relationships. They are more focused, grateful and balanced. I see that when they are present, they can actually be present. And when they are called on to perform at high levels under tremendous pressure and stress, their tanks are full enough to do so. They outperform the less "selfish" leaders.

Years later, I'd still argue that the dad in the pool had taken this concept too far. Like anything else, you need to find the right balance of taking care of yourself while you attend to the people who depend on you. But, unfortunately, most leaders neglect themselves, not others.

How about you? What do you do to take care of yourself? Do you make self-care a priority? Here are some clues that the answer may be "nope":

- People are constantly telling you that you look tired.
- You are not sleeping well.
- You are working on the urgent instead of the important and essential.
- You are resentful of people who get to have fun.
- You have lost your mojo; you don't have the energy or ideas that used to come naturally for you.
- Your wife is throwing Ambien at you.

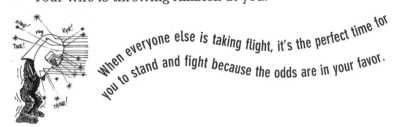

When everyone else is taking flight, it's the perfect time for you to stand and fight because the odds are in your favor.

THE POWER OF MANIACAL MEASUREMENT

> "Too many people measure how successful they are by how much money they make or the people that they associate with. In my opinion, true success should be measured by how happy you are."
>
> – Richard Branson

My bet is that you have a pretty good idea about how much money you have right now. You probably know roughly what is in your checking account, savings accounts and 401(k). But do you know how many days this year you plan on doing what makes *you* happy?

For most of us, the answer is "no." Too many leaders spend all of their time dutifully fulfilling their obligations at home and at work and neglect to make space for rejuvenating activities. The sad irony is that we "someday" the things we are working to be able to do. *Bike across the country?* Someday. *Write my novel?* Someday. *Take that fishing trip with dad?* Someday. *Learn guitar?* Someday. *Take care of myself?* Someday.

There is a fable that has grown popular among businesspeople. It shines some light on this "someday" point.

Here's the tale.

A businessman on vacation stumbles across a man on the beach laying in a hammock, strumming a guitar and singing to his kids.

The businessman asks the guy in the hammock what he does for a living, and he learns that he's a fisherman. He also learns that the waters are teaming with fish; they practically jump into your boat!

Excited and sensing opportunity, he encourages the man in the hammock to buy a bigger boat, then a fleet of boats, then build a cannery, then become super rich and successful ... so that someday he can afford to spend his days swinging in a hammock on a beach, playing his guitar and singing to his kids.

Strategically selfish Disruptors understand that "someday" is today.

What would happen if you made *your* someday start today? What would happen if you measured more than your 401(k)? What if you intentionally created the life you wanted—the life you are tirelessly working to attain?

Jack Daly is a maniacal measurement monster. Jack Daly is a Disruptor. I will tell you about his career in a second. But for now, I want to point out that Jack Daly makes sure every day of his life is rich and full of what others might put off to do "someday."

"One more test and I think we have our winner!"

Jack calls his goal setting "Life by Design." Throughout his life, he has put his goals in writing and then enlisted friends and associates to help him achieve them. He then makes a quarterly report to what he calls the board of directors of his life—five people, all trusted business associates who hold him accountable. Every year, he reviews his goals for living the life he wants and shares them in detail. Then quarterly, he looks at what went right and what went wrong, preparing for his annual report to those five people. (See the sidebar "365 Days of Goals" on pages 197–199.)

Let's take running, for example. Jack Daly ran his first marathon at the age of 46. Fifteen years ago, Jack told me he was going to run a marathon in all 50 states. He also told me he was going to run a marathon on every continent, including Antarctica. At the time, it wasn't the goals that impressed me, it was my realization that he was actually going to achieve them.
I knew this to be true because that's what Jack does. He sets goals, measures progress and completes them. Jack measures his fun.

He accomplished his goals, of course. Jack just finished his 50th marathon in his final state. Last year, Jack also ran a marathon in Antarctica, checking the box for his final continent.

But why just run when you can swim and bike too? In between all of the marathons, Jack decided to do his first triathlon at the age of 57. Since then, he has completed 15 full Ironmans and 30 half Ironmans—one on each continent. (FYI: An Ironman consists of a 2.4-mile swim, followed by a 112-mile bike ride, followed by a 26.2-mile marathon. Yowza!) Jack is on his seventh decade on the planet, and it sure seems like the guy is just getting started.

People (and I am one of them) have told Jack that his annual list contains more than some people would do in a lifetime. Jack's response to this is what you might expect: "If I were to have a tombstone, all I want on it is my name with a check mark."

Strategically selfish? Absolutely. When was the last time you sat down and selfishly made a list of the things you want to do instead of the things you think you have to do?

Selfishly setting, measuring and achieving goals has resulted in quite a résumé for Jack. Today, Jack Daly is a world-renowned sales speaker and trainer but has been successful across a broad variety of industries and leadership roles. He started his professional journey as a CPA at Arthur Andersen and rose to the CEO level of several corporations, building six companies into national firms along the way, two of which he subsequently sold to the Wall Street firms of Solomon Brothers and First Boston.

So the idea that having fun doing what you love keeps you from being successful in business is absolutely false. Ironically, I've found the opposite to be true. People who don't make room for themselves underperform at home and at work.

Did I mention that Jack Daly is also a best-selling author and has written and contributed to many books, including "Hyper Sales Growth" and "The Sales Playbook for Hyper Sales Growth"? Sheesh, enough already.

365 Days of Goals

Take a look at Jack's list of goals for last year:[3]

PERSONAL GOALS – JACK DALY

THEME: Life balance is a priority, continuing to "make a difference" as a professional speaker while enjoying more home life in southern California. Physical fitness while having fun (bucket list) and world travel is part of such balance.

A. FAMILY
1. Bonnie (wife)
2. Melissa (daughter) and family
3. Adam (son) and extended family

B. HEALTH
1. Weight (or less) by quarter: 180 – 177 – 175 – 173 (1)
2. No wine unless <180 lbs. (4 free days per month). Wine days to be less than workout days.
3. Workouts: 4 to 5 times per week / 250 per year.
4. Marathons: 49 states completed / 88 total, in quest of 50 states / all continents / 100 overall. Continents to be completed in May. 50 states to be completed in October.
   a. Disney half – January
   b. Surf City – February
   c. D.C. – March
   d. Great Wall of China – May
   e. Atlantic City – October
5. Triathlons: Asia Ironman will complete all continents, with Malaysia in November.
   a. Oceanside 70.3 – April
   b. Maine 70.3 – August
   c. Malaysia full – November
6. Swim yards: 72,000 / 24 hours / 2 hours per month
7. Run: 700 miles / 132 hours / 11 hours per month

---

[3] This list almost made me want to buy Viagra…almost.

365 Days of Goals (continued)

8. Bike: 2,500 miles / 144 hours / 12 hours per month
9. Bike stationary: 1,500 miles / 108 hours / 9 hours per month
10. Strength / weight workouts: 72 per year / 6 per month
11. Rowing: 48 hours / 4 hours per month
12. Blood platelet donations: 6 per year
13. Doctors: medical December / dentist 3 times per year / eyes summer / skin May
14. Floss daily
15. Water: 1/2 gallon daily
16. Sleep: 6 hours nightly

C. QUALITY OF LIFE / TRAVEL / VACATIONS
1. Mexico / Cabo – February
2. Murphy family in California – February
3. Peru / Chile / Machu Picchu – March
4. Family cruise – Caribbean – April
5. Hamilton Island, Australia – April
6. China / Thailand – May
7. Palm Springs – June
8. California Beach week – August
9. Iovines in California – August
10. South Carolina golf with Rick – September
11. Nova Scotia – September

D. VISITS WITH THE YOUNG FAMILY
1. March – D.C.
2. April – cruise
3. June – Palm Springs
4. July – Charlottesville
5. October – Atlantic City
6. December – Christmas

E. GOLF TOP 100
1. 92 total
2. Goal of 4 more in 2017

F. EVENTS
1. Mexico/Cabo
2. Adam wedding
3. China tours / Great Wall / Thailand
4. Malaysia / Ironman
5. Nova Scotia / golf

365 Days of Goals (continued)

6. Ireland / golf
7. Carolina golf / Rick
8. Hollywood sign / June
9. Blimp / June
10. Indoor skydive
11. Segway
12. Bikram hot yoga
13. AcroYoga
14. Publish 2 new books – Shavitz and Bailey
15. Several photo books

G. HOUSEHOLD
1. Sell LaQuinta house
2. New car – Jack
3. Investment management review: 2 times per year

H. BALANCE/PERSONAL DEVELOPMENT
1. Books: 30 per year
2. Movies: 60 per year
3. Magazines: 12 monthly
4. Manage / monitor sleep: 3 nights

Quarter	1	2	3	4	TOTAL 2016 Plan/Act
Business	29	30	27	25	111
Home	47	35	48	43	173
Fun	14	26	17	24	81
Total	90	91	92	92	365
Meals at home	30	25	36	26	117

I. FOOTNOTES
1. A few goals specifically identified as:
   a. Nonnegotiable
   b. Most difficult
   c. Most important

No surprise, Jack managed to check the box next to nearly every goal for the year.

Back to striking the right balance. I once asked Jack how his wife, Bonnie, put up with all his goals and the time they ate up. It was obvious to me that all of his goal setting and achieving took him away from his family and his home. I wondered aloud if it made his wife crazy.

Jack responded that Bonnie was his high school sweetheart. And she saw early on what Jack needed to achieve to feed his soul. Besides, Jack had goals for family too. And he made sure Bonnie was on the top of the list as you saw in the sidebar.

As Jack and Bonnie reflected upon their lives together, it was clear that together they had seen more and done more than most couples would accomplish in 10 lifetimes. Jack has the checklists to prove it.

We should all be so lucky.

> When it comes to innovation,
> I am bearish on bears and bullish
> on bulls. I think you should be too.

SOME DISRUPTOR RESOLUTIONS TO CONSIDER

In late December of every year, many of us start to consider New Year's resolutions. Some of us will vow to eat less, exercise more, live in the moment and be more grateful. You may even decide to bury the hatchet with the family member who makes you so crazy.

But have you ever wondered what kind of resolutions business Disruptors make and *keep*?

The emphasis is on the word "keep." Sadly, like our personal goals, we often make them (year after year) with sincere intent, only to see them quickly fall by the wayside, as we revert to (bad) habits that we have vowed to break.

So how about the Disruptors and their resolutions? As I have journeyed through the C-suite of Russell 2000 companies, I've noticed how the most accomplished people just seem to identify important things and consistently get them done.

If you study balanced and successful Disruptors long enough, you start to pick up on the resolutions they seem to consistently make (and keep).

Here are 10 of my favorites:

1. **Spend more time on the not-to-do list.**
   Strategy is the art of sacrifice. That's why you may want to create a larger clearing for what really matters by first identifying and then avoiding what matters the least. Your time is a treasure to be invested. Creating a list of things that you are not going to do allows you to invest more of your treasured time on the few things that matter the most.

2. **Essential first, digital second.**
   What's the first thing you do in the morning? For many of us, it is looking at email or social media posts. We wake up with a renewed mind and spirit, ready to take on the world, and then we immediately allow ourselves to be distracted by an insignificant message. Instead of doing that, wake up, take on the most important task of the day, and then (and only then) hit the email.

3. **Resolve to think about "who" instead of "what."**
   Do you work for a "what" business or for a "who" business? Successful companies run the risk of focusing too much on their current products and distributors (the "what") thus losing sight of the constant and dramatically changing needs of their customer base (the "who"). Insurance, pharma, health care and higher education often listen too much to their agents, doctors and professors. The real innovation starts with the end consumer. (See Chapter 9.)

4. **Resolve to find your purpose.**
   As my friend Simon Sinek will tell you: "People don't buy what you do, they buy why you do it." Starting a career, a company or any kind of journey that is based firmly on your purpose is foundational to success and happiness. If you don't know your company's purpose or even your own, finding one is the worthiest of resolutions. (See Chapter 9.)

5. **Resolve to support a cause.**
   If you're reading this, chances are you are one of the rare people who know how to start things. Fortunately, there are people like you who have already started causes that make the world better—they feed the hungry; they save the rain forest; they fight cancer; they do good things. There is virtually a cause for everyone, and contributing will make your year happier. I promise.

6. **Resolve to invent more choices.**
   Here's a secret that happy people know that I learned from my friend Dr. Dan Baker: "You can't feel grateful and fearful at the same time." And one certain way to become afraid is to feel trapped by any situation. The remedy is choice. The more choices you feel you have, the less trapped—and happier—you will feel. So this year, resolve to do a bit of brainstorming every time you feel unhappy.

7. **Resolve to find a yin for your yang.**
   Walt Disney had Roy Disney, Steve Jobs had Steve Wozniak and Orville Wright had Wilbur Wright. Wherever there is great innovation, there is a dreamer and an operator—an Idea Monkey and a Ringleader. First, determine where your passions lie, then go find an equally passionate partner, then go change the world. (See Chapter 10.)

8. **Resolve to get outside your jar.**
   You can't read the label when you are sitting inside the jar. The sad irony of being an expert is that it keeps you from seeing possibility. After all, you know what works, what doesn't, what you can afford and what's been tried in the

past. Instead of relying only on your expertise, learn how to find other experts solving similar challenges to the ones you are facing. Go ask them what you may be missing.

9. **Resolve to be the creator.**

   What is the outcome you want? What stands in your way? How do you overcome these obstacles? These three simple questions will keep you from being victimized by any situation. Creators change the world. Victims just bitch about stuff. (See Chapter 4.)

10. **Plan vacations (now).**

   To quote John Lennon: "Life is what happens when you are not paying attention." Unfortunately for many of us, we let this become true. Do yourself a favor and plan your vacations for the next year today. Be a little selfish. I promise you that the days around your vacation will fill in nicely. I also promise you that you'll have something to look forward to, and the life that happens during your vacations will be precious.

Here's to the Disruptor in all of us. Now, go forth and make a positive dent in the universe.

DISRUPTOR TAKEAWAYS AND HACKS

1. **Make four-sided goals.** Serial entrepreneur David Rich sets aside a day every quarter to set goals. To make sure he is being strategically selfish (emphasis on strategic), he sets goals in four categories: self, business, family and community. This approach allows him to take care of himself AND the things that are most important to him in a balanced, proactive way.

DISRUPTOR TAKEAWAYS AND HACKS (cont.)

2. Take an IQ staycation. Have you noticed you have some of your biggest ideas when you are relaxing or checked out mentally? Science supports the use of regular mental breaks to create space for big ideas. It turns out that even your brain needs vacations.

Eileen McDonnell, CEO of Penn Mutual, knew she needed to keep most of her mental vacations very local. As a single, 44-year-old executive, she decided the time was right to adopt a child–which meant being home as much as possible. Read: Golfing and marathon training were not mental break options.

Eileen keeps her staycations simple, mindless and fun. Her tactics include reading *People* magazine, watching Wheel of Fortune, and helping her daughter groom her horse. These indulgences are intentional and strategic. They have afforded her the energy to take care of her family, herself and her company, which has risen 219 positions (so far) on the *Fortune* 1000 list.

So, the next time you have the urge to binge on Netflix, cut yourself some slack. Your brain just needs a vacation.

(Take a break for some doodling!)

Chapter 12

Dream, Drive And Deliver

"Leadership might as well be a law of physics. Show me a negative team and I will show you a negative leader."
— Col. Bernard (Bernie) Banks

Can a Disruptor be a good leader?

Here's news that won't stop the presses (especially if you have read the book straight through): Disruptive leaders are flawed human beings. Spend some time with a Disruptor and it will become abundantly clear that their superhero strengths are often mirrored by dumbfounding weaknesses that can hinder their ability to lead. These weaknesses often mar their legacies.

Quite often a Disruptor's weaknesses are caused by what Carl Jung, who founded analytical psychiatry, described as the leader's "shadow self." That's his term for the hidden, dark side of a person, a part that is unknown to them. (See page 28).

According to Jung, the shadow is both instinctive and irrational and is prone to projection, meaning that the person's (hidden from them) personal inferiority is seen and labeled as a perceived moral deficiency in someone else, even though the person cannot see that same trait in himself.

As I researched this book, it was interesting to discover how the Disruptor's "shadow selves" were smack dab in the middle of their most epic failures. For example, Steve Jobs made a career out of taking on (and defeating) the bully big boys of the industry, and the list was quite impressive: Microsoft, AT&T, Sony, Random House, IBM, Nokia....

This David versus Goliath chip on his shoulder became the rallying cry for many of his most notable breakthroughs. But behind closed doors, he became the bully, famously making employees (grown men and women) cry as he berated them for being too slow, too stupid or too unoriginal. The best Disruptors recognize their weaknesses and spend a lifetime learning and becoming more aware of these shadows. But history is rich with leaders who were blind to their weaknesses or, worse, saw them as an intractable part of their fabric.

ARE YOU A SCORPION?

In the parable of the scorpion and the frog, a scorpion pleads with a frog to swim him to the other side of a river, assuring the wary frog that he'd be stupid to hurt him because they would both drown if he did. This logic makes perfect sense to the frog, so he begins to swim to the other side with the scorpion on his back.

Just before they make landfall, the frog feels the sting of the scorpion. Baffled, the dying frog asks the scorpion why he has stung him, to which his passenger replies, "Because I am a scorpion."

A year after being elected, President Trump attended the heavily partisan Conservative Political Action Conference (CPAC) where he read a poem[1] that he had regularly performed at his campaign events. It's about a woman who rescues a snake who ends up biting and killing her. In Trump's telling, the snake is supposed to represent immigrants, but to the moderates watching, he might as well have been talking about his own demons:

---

[1] Although Trump described it as a poem, it is actually a lyric by Oscar Brown, Jr. who recorded it. Johnny Rivers later covered it and had a hit with it.

On her way to work one morning
Down the path along side the lake
A tender hearted woman saw a poor half frozen snake
His pretty colored skin had been all frosted with the dew
"Poor thing," she cried, "I'll take you in and I'll take care of you"

She wrapped him all cozy in a comforter of silk
And laid him by her fireside with some honey and some milk
She hurried home from work that night and soon as she arrived
She found that pretty snake she'd taken to had be revived

She clutched him to her bosom, "You're so beautiful," she cried
"But if I hadn't brought you in by now you might have died"
She stroked his pretty skin again and kissed and held him tight
Instead of saying thanks, the snake gave her a vicious bite

"I saved you," cried the woman
"And you've bitten me, but why?
You know your bite is poisonous and now I'm going to die"
"Oh shut up, silly woman," said the reptile with a grin
"You knew damn well I was a snake before you took me in"

If you consider yourself a Disruptor, how often are you the scorpion or the snake in these parables?

Unfortunately, the greatest Disruptors are often like scorpions, unable to resist giving in to their darkest urges or most basic instincts.

History shows what I said at the beginning of the chapter, that Disruptors are often far from perfect. For example, Bill Clinton's name will be forever tied to Monica Lewinsky and Donald Trump's to "the Russia investigation" and sexual misconduct.

In sports, Tiger Woods and Lance Armstrong are now seen as notorious as they are gifted. And in business, Steve Jobs and Ray Kroch have well-earned reputations as being great visionaries, even while being saddled with what seemed to be a stunning lack of empathy because of the way they bullied their way to success.

WHICH DISRUPTOR CAN TEACH US THE MOST?

Years ago, I was complaining to my friend and mentor Rick Voirin about Jack Welch. I had just seen him on television promoting his new book. By his side was his mistress, turned third wife. I wondered out loud how the TV segment made his first and second wife and his children feel. I told Rick that my judgment about Welch's personal life—and that's what it was: "judgy"—made it hard for me to learn from the former chairman and CEO of GE, who truly was a remarkable businessman. Rick's sage reply: "Mike, judge the medicine, not the vessel."

> ## "A small body of determined spirits fired by an unquenchable faith in their mission can alter the course of history."
> ### Mahatma Gandhi[2]

It turns out that it is very easy for people to confuse the ability to change organizations—and even countries—through leadership with the ability to do it through disruption, especially if that disruption is imbued with the negative traits of the leader's shadow self. Let me give you an example of the confusion I am talking about.

I was flying to a business meeting with an associate when he told me he didn't think I was a very good leader. (Ouch!) Since up until that point I had trusted his opinion, I asked him why. He explained that it was because he'd never seen me yell at anyone. In his experience, leaders had an edge that was best expressed through explosive decibels, with veins bulging in their foreheads. He was serious; he was looking for my inner marine sergeant to come out and play.

---

[2] Just to drive home the point, I'll play the Hitler card here. He talked about faith too: "I believe today that my conduct is in accordance with the will of the Almighty Creator." I can think of no better example of a Disruptor who turned out to be the shi**iest of leaders. Regardless, can we learn something from both of them? We'd better be able to.

I was stunned. I had never linked the volume of one's voice to good leadership.

In hindsight, I believe my associate was looking for a Disruptor, not a leader. When I probed a little, I learned that his father was prone to yelling, as were his prior two employers.

In contrast, my dad got quiet when he was upset. In critical moments, his voice would get even lower and more measured. This was the way he made sure he had your attention. My father retired as Navy captain. He drove a ship. He fought in a war and led men. He then spent more than 35 years running baking facilities for Keebler/Kellogg's. Upon retirement, he volunteered to operate the parish where he had been a deacon for more than 20 years and a retirement community that was down the street.

My dad was a leader because people followed him, not because he yelled or made subordinates feel bad. Again, too often we mistake disruptive behavior for strategic leadership.

Without being too political—because many of you will stop reading—it has been fascinating to watch how America is judging its leaders lately. You hear phrases like "He says it like it is" or "He knows how to win" or "He gets things done" often to rationalize behavior that seems less than "leaderly." These people are talking about affective disruptive behavior, not strong leadership.

HOW TO BE A DISRUPTOR AND A GOOD LEADER

The rapid pace of change, politics and my lesson in perception at 30,000 feet got me thinking about great leadership—more specifically, what the best leaders I know have in common. So while leaders come in all shapes and sizes, in my humble opinion, you simply cannot be a great, or even a good leader (Disruptor or not) unless you embody the following three traits:

1. You must be worthy of trust.

Recently when challenged about going over an agreed-upon time limit for video game play, my teenage son said, "Would you rather I just lie to you about the time I am online?"

My response was simple: "No, I would rather you did what you said you were going to do. I need to be able to trust you."

Good leaders are trustworthy; they are worthy of trust. If they tell you they are going to do something, they do it. If they can't do it for some reason, they apologize and tell you why.

Honesty and trust are the fundamental ingredients in integrity. According to the *Economist*, both workers and CEOs rated integrity as the most essential leadership trait. If you are trustworthy, it likely means you are a person of high integrity.

I've never, ever met a great leader with low integrity.

Want to know if someone is trustworthy? A great indication of trustworthiness is how a leader perceives the actions of people around him. If the leader does not trust others (for example, if he or she always thinks someone is trying to take advantage of him), it is likely the leader is not trustworthy. They presume that others are going to act badly, like they would in a similar situation. (Think back to our discussion of the shadow self.)

It gets worse. That old cliché is right: The fish really does stink from the head down. A leader who is not trustworthy creates an organization full of people who do not trust each other.

This leads us to our next characteristic.

2. You must be accountable.

President Truman famously had a sign on his desk that read: "The buck stops here." Leadership is messy. Mistakes happen. Good leaders first take responsibility for mishaps and then work with their teams to assess what happened and build a better strategy for the future.

In response to questions about the controversial (and failed) U.S. military raid in Yemen in January 2017, Gen. Joseph Votel, commander of U.S. Central Command, told the Senate Armed Services Committee: "I am responsible for this mission. I accept the responsibility for this. We lost a lot on this operation. We lost a valued operator (Chief Petty Officer William 'Ryan' Owens, a Navy Seal). We had people wounded. We caused civilian casualties, we lost an expensive aircraft."

The military uses a practice called an after action review (AAR) to ensure learning and future optimal performance. The first step of the AAR is for the leader to take full responsibility for the event and make it clear that it is about learning and NOT assigning blame.

In other words, the leader must first be accountable before asking his/her team for areas of improvement. It is the only way to ensure learning over fear and loathing.

A typical AAR includes the following questions:

- What was supposed to happen?
- What actually happened?
- Why were there differences?
- What worked, what didn't and why?
- What might we do differently next time?

Said differently, real leaders don't look to blame; they look to learn. When things go wrong, they don't get furious; they get curious.

This leads us to our last leadership characteristic.

Surround yourself with curious experts

3. You are a learner, not a knower.

Being a lifelong learner is perhaps the trickiest leadership trait to retain. Most people believe that as you mature as a leader, you are expected to be an expert, which means you know all or at least most of the answers. I'll admit, this is what I thought as a younger person. It turns out, I was wrong (again).

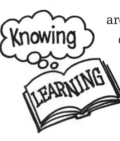

The best leaders understand that questions are more powerful than answers. And it's pretty difficult to ask good questions when you think you know all the answers. If you think you do, you quickly turn into the man behind the curtain; you think of yourself as The Great and Powerful Oz, but your people sense that you are not and fear a trap.

Here are the three questions leaders ask their teams:

1. What is the outcome we need to make happen?
2. What stands in our way?
3. Who has already figured this out?

As mentioned earlier, these questions will help turn teams into creators instead of victims. They will naturally stoke the sense of wonder and curiosity found in the "crazy ones." The best disruptive leaders intuitively understand that this curiosity and boldness is at the heart of their own genius. Because "…people who are crazy enough to think they can change the world, are the ones that do."

The strategic conversations that flow from these questions allow people (your peers, friends and employees) to learn from a great leader (you).

Now, go change the world.

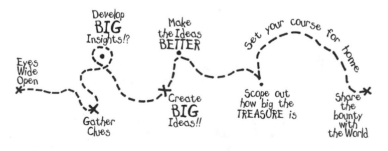

Your Superhero Power

"What have I done?!"

I began the book on a personal note. Let me end the same way.

When I was a kid, parent-teacher conferences didn't go so well for my folks. On a good day, I was charitably described as a highly imaginative and creative student.

But alas, most days were not good days. From the first grade on, my poor parents were regularly treated to a myriad of disappointing reports about my progress as a student. They got to hear that I daydreamed and I imitated people and drew caricatures of my teachers.

I was bored, so I was doodling, cracking jokes and doing impressions when I was supposed to be paying attention.[1] My teachers reported that I didn't seem all that concerned about learning. They thought I had some real potential, but I clearly wasn't interested in living up to it.

My poor parents were flummoxed.

What made this really frustrating for my mom and dad was that they both had been exceptional students. They had worked hard, gotten good grades, graduated at the top of their high school classes, and earned scholarships to learn some more—my dad at Notre Dame and my mom at St. Mary's College just across the street. They had played by the rules and thrived. So my behavior completely baffled

---

[1] I now get paid for all of these. Oh, the irony.

them. How could this alien have sprung from their loins? Whatever happened to that great Midwestern expression "plant corn, get corn?"

Perhaps their first encounter with each other in South Bend provides a small clue. As freshmen, they were attending a mock Republican convention, during which my dad had gotten a bit too enthusiastic and was talking too much. (Mom, Dad, does that sound like anyone you know?)

My mom—never one to mince words—kicked his chair and said, "Excuse me, would you please shut up?"

It was love at first snipe.

A decade later, they had spawned an enigma, thus proving two things:

1. God has an awesome sense of humor, and

2. He never gives us a cross we cannot bear.

Despite their frustration, my parents were optimistic, undaunted and resourceful. Rather than give up on their "cross," they turned to a time-tested strategy: the Catholic school system. They figured that if they could not break me of my disruptive habits, a legion of nuns and priests armed with guilt, prayer and detentions would surely be able to save my flawed soul.

It was not to be. Candles were lit, prayers were said, tears were shed and detentions were served. But as I approached high school, I was steadfast in my jackassedness.[2]

I was unaffected by all attempts to save my academic career and had driven more than one nun into early retirement by the time I barely graduated eighth grade.

Did somebody say high school? That sounded fun too. What could possibly go wrong?

---

[2] For the record, "jackassedness" is a word. Look it up; you'll see a picture of me in the eighth grade.

It was at this point that I won my first major argument with my dad. (This was a big win because part of the scholarship he had received to attend Notre Dame was for debate, so to win any argument with him, you actually had to do your homework.)

He and my mom wanted to stick with the plan and send me to Marion Catholic High School. Their reasoning was simple: I didn't feel that guilty about anything yet, so the nuns still had plenty of work to do.

But I argued that I should be allowed to attend Homewood Flossmoor, the public high school in Flossmoor, a Chicago suburb. I was interested in the arts and was thinking that maybe—just maybe—I could be a pretty good architect, cartoonist or designer. At the time, Marion had three art courses while Homewood Flossmoor had more than 40. "Case closed," I said. (See previous "jackassedness.")

G. Michael Maddock
Age 11

My father could not argue with my reasoning. He also liked to hear that I was interested in something—ANYTHING—related to school. So he relented, under one condition...that I attend Teen Encounter, a Christian Youth group that met weekly.

Teen Encounter was run by Father Joe Ruiz, a family friend.

Father Joe looked like a clean-shaven Santa Claus caught out of uniform. He laughed like Fozzy Bear from "The Muppet Show" and had some new age ideas, including teaching my class how to meditate. I liked Joe and he seemed mildly charmed by my playful antics. So saying "yes" to my dad's condition of attending Teen Encounter was a no-brainer (particularly considering there were girls in Teen Encounter, and I was starting to really like girls).

During the summer between eighth grade and my freshman year, I was on a weekend retreat with the Teen Encounter group. We were off in the country at an old estate and, as usual, I was making an ass out of myself. I was running back and forth, horsing around with my buddies and doing everything I could to get the attention of any girl willing to look my way.

At the time, Father Joe was sitting in the corner. He appeared to be watching a tennis match, his head moving back and forth as he tracked me and my friends bouncing off the walls. About then, he waved me over.

I sat down next to him. I was sweaty, distracted and wanted to end the conversation quickly.

"Mike, look at me a second. This is important." Joe paused until he saw I was temporarily focused on him. "I've known you now for what, a couple years?" I nodded, hoping he'd get right to the point. "And I'd say I know you pretty well. I've noticed something really interesting. You wanna know what I've noticed?"

He could see that I wasn't really that interested in what he had noticed. So he took an uncomfortably long pause to make sure I was paying attention.

"I've noticed you can be a real a**hole."

Time stood still. I was absolutely stunned and sat there looking at Joe with my jaw open.

He stared at me, unblinking, as my eyes welled up with tears. He now had my attention. And he could see that his words had really cut me.

I'd never heard a priest swear. Ever. And Joe knew it. He had skillfully broken through my distraction and landed a meaningful punch.

Ouch.[3]

---

[3] I really would have preferred a ruler to the wrist.

Here's the thing...he was absolutely right. I could be an a**hole. At the time, in addition to my jackassedness, my insecurity sometimes led me to rely on cleverness to make others feel small so I could feel big.

Joe saw through my insecurity. He knew the reason I didn't try at school, in part, was because I was afraid I might fail. When you don't try, you can continue to tell yourself that if you really wanted to, you could accomplish anything.

But then Joe went on to say that he'd also noticed my big heart. He said that he had watched me defend kids with learning disabilities and use humor to bring shy kids into the fold. He told me that when I wanted to, I could be a pretty nice kid.

He challenged me to stop being a jerk and be the guy he saw when nobody was looking. He told me to stop being such an a**hole, that I was better than that.

In my small brain, I heard him telling me that I had a superhero power: the talent to see things differently and force unexpected outcomes—one that I must use for good, not evil.

For the first time, I saw disruption as a good thing.

Joe's words changed me. He had somehow managed to change my trajectory with a well-timed challenge, delivered with extreme candor and love.

We all have a superhero power, but not everyone benefits from a Yoda-like challenger named Father Joe.

The lesson for Disruptors is pretty simple: You have a superhero power, perhaps more than one. But as we have seen throughout, our greatest strengths are also our greatest weaknesses. This book was created to help you use your superhero power for the good of the whole.

I believe all Disruptors should have a personal manifesto to keep them focused on what is truly important to them.

I leave you with mine.

Mike Maddock Manifesto (has a nice ring to it)

I am full of wonder; I am wonder-full. I am a believer, a dreamer and a wide-eyed risk-taker. And you can count on me to lean into adversity, start with yes and believe in your dreams, so you can be wonder-full too.

My purpose is to inspire and empower curiosity.

I believe that childlike curiosity and sense of wonder are what give leaders and organizations an unfair competitive advantage over our rapidly changing future.

I believe that "you can't read the label when you are sitting inside the jar."

I believe that the longer you have been working on a challenge, relationship or industry, the more your well-earned expertise keeps you from seeing new possibility.

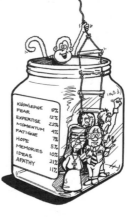

I believe that most mature organizations are perfectly engineered to kill any new product, service or business model that threatens their legacy offerings.

I believe in orchestrating "Napster Moments." I believe in connecting business leaders with someone with no business being in their business who is about to put them out of business.

I believe that pioneers replace the words "problems" and "failing" with "possibilities" and "learning."

I believe that people support what they create. I believe that your team must be fully enrolled in the innovation process in order for new products, services — or the culture itself — to thrive.

I believe that serendipity can be engineered.

I believe that a truly relevant new product, service or business model is the best example of a brand promise well kept.

I believe in dreamers and believers because they are the ones who make world-changing ideas happen.

I believe that the size of the insight is predictive of the impact of the idea.

I believe that true innovation is insight driven while more common invention is idea driven.

I believe that the innovation process depends on the delicate balance between brilliant divergent and convergent thinkers. I believe that there are proven processes and tools with which to keep this balance in check.

I believe that evolutionary ideas are best grown from within mature organizations and revolutionary, disruptive ideas are best imported, invested in or avoided completely.

I believe that the proper mix of brutal reality and quantifiable possibility is the best way to enroll the C-suite.

I believe that small and midsized companies are more capable of innovating because they are not fighting the inertia of quarterly earnings calls and impatient shareholders.

I believe in taking a stake in the outcome.

I believe that if you think something is impossible, you are absolutely correct.

I believe that optimists find more treasure.

I believe that CEOs who are only a few years from retirement rarely support innovation or dramatic change.

I don't believe in retirement.

Mike Maddock Manifesto (continued)

I believe that we have moved from a B2B to a B2C to a B2Me world and the most evolved companies listen closely to their customer's, customer's customer.

I believe that Idea Monkeys are dangerous unless partnered with a great Ringleader. I believe that Ringleaders are too predictable if they go it alone.

I believe that my assumptions may be wrong, and I want everyone around me to challenge them.

I believe that the practice of innovation and the practice of entrepreneurship are ridiculously similar.

I believe in the ability of one person, with the right idea at the right time, to change the world.

I believe in "love at first sight."

I believe that the best gift parents can give their kids is gratefulness. The second best gift is the belief that they can make a difference in the world.

I believe in the Butterfly Effect.

I believe that fear is the enemy of possibility.

I believe that God is the perfect creator.

Be sure to read our other books.

Free the Idea Monkey...
to focus on what matters most!

Striking the balance between imagination and execution

Are you more like Walt Disney or Roy Disney? Do you lead through inspired ideas or precise execution? Examine the most innovative firms and you will see they have mastered the balance between the visionaries and the operators. This book was written to help you and your team do the same.

Flirting With the Uninterested –
Innovating in a "Sold, Not Bought" Category

Applying innovation to the insurance industry

Do you suspect that there is some brilliant, forward-thinking entre-preneur in a garage somewhere about to reinvent your industry? More important, when you raise the issue, do those around you look at you like you're crazy? You are not crazy. The insurance industry IS ripe for reinvention, and the paradigm Is ready for a shift. "Flirting With the Uninterested" is our contribution to help leaders like you begin the journey to innovating in a "sold, not bought" category.

Brand New: Solving the Innovation Paradox

The innovation process

How does David beat Goliath? How do the best brands in the world create customers for life? What is the highest indicator of future profitability according to many on Wall Street? The answer to all three questions is the same: by creating game-changing new products. "Brand New" explains in step-by-step fashion what you need to do (and what you should never do) to innovate effectively.